IT WASN'T ALL BAD!

A GLIMPSE INTO 37 YEARS OF POLICING IN
COUNTIES MANUKAU

MICHAEL MORGAN

For Wendy, Jonathan & Anthony. Thank you for your love, support, patience and understanding.

"All rights reserved. No part of this book may be reproduced in any form or by any electronic or mechanical means, including information storage and retrieval systems, without written permission from the author, except in the case of a reviewer, who may quote brief passages embodied in critical articles or in a review. Trademarked names appear throughout this book. Rather than use a trademark symbol with every occurrence of a trademarked name, names are used in an editorial fashion, with no intention of infringement of the respective owner's trademark. The information in this book is distributed on an "as is" basis, without warranty. Although every precaution has been taken in the preparation of this work, neither the author nor the publisher shall have any liability to any person or entity with respect to any loss or damage caused or alleged to be caused directly or indirectly by the information contained in this book."

CONTENTS

Preface 6
1. What am I doing here? 7
2. Let's get this party started! 31
3. A change of pace. 55
4. What do we do now Sarge? 69
5. What's this Prosecuting lark all about? 82
6. I think I still want to be a prosecutor…in fact I know that I do. 98
7. The return of the prodigal son 108
8. Are you looking for something? 113
9. I'm not getting into a scrap with him! 117
10. Run, Prosecutor, Run! 122
11. Did it hurt? 130
12. Can you hum it for me please Sarge? 134
13. How many zeros was that? 139
14. Does anyone here drive legally Sarge? 146
15. Everything is rosy? 151
16. But boss, there's no hole at the bottom of the funnel. .. 159
17. Looks can be deceiving. 168
18. I'll take an away mission please. 174
19. Communication is always the key. 182
20. A tale of two high profile cases. 190
21. Better work stories, too right. 201

22. And it all came down to this…. the conclusion to my hopeless opus. 218

Epilogue..228

About the author:..231

Photographic Acknowledgements:.....................................232

PREFACE

Some stories don't need to be told and this is probably one of them. My Police career was neither significant nor important. Many Officers have done far greater things than I. Their stories make mine pale into insignificance. However, I did stick with it for 37 years and that should count for something. I was proud of some of the things I achieved, particularly in the role of Prosecutor.

Readers will note that very few participants are actually named, unless they are celebrities or it would be rude not to. I simply don't want the drama of upsetting someone or forgetting others. I'm also mindful that in some instances I'm protecting what may be perceived as misdeeds, statute of limitations and all. I'm also confident that those of you who were around at the time will have little difficulty in putting the pieces together.

You can be assured that each of the stories are true. However, some are slightly embellished for effect, but not so much as to destroy factual integrity.

I really enjoyed my time with New Zealand Police. It's a pity that another Government Department left a sour taste at the end. No ongoing resentment...yeah right!

That being said, come with me now on this mildly interesting adventure, after all….IT WASN'T ALL BAD!

1. WHAT AM I DOING HERE?

Great, you've chosen to come along with me for the ride and a glimpse into 37 years of Policing in the Counties Manukau District, so I guess the journey starts now. It all began on 19 January 1981 when sixty, mainly eighteen-year-olds settled into Barracks 10 and 11 of the Trentham Police College, Wellington. Well not really, as prior to this date there had been months of pre-selection tests and interviews, both mental and physical. It all lead to thirteen of us from Auckland boarding the overnight train at the Central Train Station and making the slow journey to Wellington. The alarm bells should have started ringing then. If this outfit was so tight that it couldn't afford to fly us, then it might have been a bad omen for the future. In reality it may have been a test. The last thing the overseeing instructor said to us before we departed unaccompanied was, "Don't drink any alcohol", which of course for us was illegal anyway, the legal age being twenty in those days.

Upon arrival at Trentham one of the first things I noticed was just how big some of these guys were. I was a tad over 6 feet and weighed about 90 kg (note the mixed measurements - something quite common with my generation). In this group of sixty my stature was decidedly average. I have this vivid memory of hearing a thumping sound coming down the barrack hallway.

Looking out I saw the largest of the Cadets who was about 6 feet 8 and around 120 kg bouncing a basketball towards me. Probably only eclipsed by the time that I happened to see Manu Vatuvei walking down a narrow hallway in the Manukau Police Station many years later. Sadly, the big Cadet was one of only two who would not graduate, eleven months later.

I wasn't a stranger to all of my new colleagues. I was joined on the intake by Dave (later to be more widely referred to as Tracker). We had been at Otahuhu College together for a couple of years and were also teammates in the First XV.

It soon became apparent that our time spent training as Police Cadets was going to be quite unusual on a number of fronts. The first thing that we were told was that the three sections of twenty of us, quite simply named A, B and C were collectively the "Prince of Wales 25th Cadet Wing". Each Wing that trained at the Police College, both Cadets (under 19 years) and Recruits (over 19 years) were assigned a Wing patron. The people who agreed to be patron and thus have their name assigned to the Wing were usually notable New Zealanders, often with some connection to law enforcement or exemplary service to the community. It was then explained to us that the Trentham Police College would be closing in March 1981 and that we would be moving to the brand new, state of the art Police College at Papakowhai, Porirua. The opening of the college was to take place on 1 April 1981 to coincide with the royal visit of HRH Prince Charles, the Prince of Wales.

He had agreed to be our Wing patron, hence the name attached to our Wing.

First though, a slight diversion to discuss hazing, which is an age-old tradition amongst most organised groups. It's thought that giving the newbies a bit of a wind-up is good for team building and morale. Modern thinking of course recognises that there is a very fine line between hazing and bullying, to the extent that it is now generally frowned upon. In the 1980s though it was alive and well in the New Zealand Police. We had heard all sorts of horror stories involving violent kidnap and firearm discharges, hopefully with blanks. Whether they were urban legend or actually occurred I don't know, but the word was that you needed to be on your guard. Because we were the only Wing in for training for much of the year we didn't have to worry about an attack from any Recruits. There was talk of a reverse haze upon the instructors. Word had been received that previous Wings had taken action during the weekly room inspections. Instructors were known to don white gloves and to wipe their hands along surfaces in the room in search of dirt. Legend states that a previous Cadet had smeared a line of black nugget on the underside of his bed frame. When the glove came up black, apparently it was a huge joke. As I say, there was talk of having a go at this, but to my knowledge none of our guys had the guts to put that one into action.

On the final weekend before the shift to Porirua a couple of enterprising Cadets did manage to reassemble two of their colleagues' rooms on the roof of one of the barracks. Quite an achievement, but I didn't really get the point of all of the effort that it took. When we shifted to Porirua you had to be careful heading down the pathway from the Residential Block to the Administration Block. Some landscaper had thought that it would be pleasant to the eye to leave a small natural lake in place there. All the Cadets could think of was throwing other Cadets into it.

I don't know how this occurred, but it certainly happened. After we had returned from Springbok tour duty, which I will discuss in more detail later, we had the first opportunity to get to know the new Recruit Wing, who were to become known as "Green Squad". Probably green because they didn't know anything, but a squad nonetheless. Anyway, they began to get a bit lippy believing that they were somehow superior to us. Remember that we had royalty on our side, I haven't a clue who their patron was. It got to the stage that some of our crew decided to declare war upon our rivals, as throwing some of them into the lake just wasn't satisfying enough. It still amazes me, but someone managed to get the local fire brigade involved and a van duly arrived with a number of high-pressure hoses. The fireman helpfully plugged them all into the main water supply and the war began. It sounds quite funny but in reality, other than taking out quite a few Recruits and their rooms, a fair bit of damage was caused. The protagonists were called to account and it really looked as though some might get their marching orders. I can only speculate at the reasoning, but the Commandant decided that a stern talking to was all that was required. The kind old Sir thankfully saw it as some young people who had served their Department well just letting off some steam. Suffice to say the groups got on pretty well after that, except 'stacking' of course. You never knew when it was going to happen but it was most likely to occur in the recreation lounges. An unruly mob would spy a lonesome Cadet or Recruit and utter the magic word "Stack". The poor unfortunate would then find themselves under a mass of bodies not wildly dissimilar to a maul in rugby but with more passion. Stay tuned for Chapter 2 which includes the haze by Section 3 Otahuhu on me, not being one of my finer moments.

Over the next few years, it became a discussion point amongst Officers, generally over a beer or two, whether you were trained at Trentham (i.e., real cops) or at Club Med Porirua (inferior beings). The Prince of Wales 25th Cadet Wing had the opportunity to experience both worlds, although it is fair to acknowledge that we did not endure a Wellington winter from the confines of the Trentham barracks, which I'm told was a joy to behold. The alarm bells should also have started to ring again when our Wing, which was the only one in residence, was used as cheap labour over a weekend to complete the move to Porirua. Truckload after truckload of furniture and other assorted items found their way over the Haywards Hill. One of our guys lost a couple of teeth when he failed to stop in time when carrying a large cabinet but Health and Safety didn't seem to be a concern in those days.

A major piece of additional news for us though shortly after arrival, was that the opening of the College on 1 April 1981 was going to be a major event, hosted by the Police

Commissioner and the Prime Minister (Robert Muldoon) to impress their guest, HRH Prince Charles. This was followed up with the advice that our Wing would have pride of place when marching onto the parade ground, be inspected by the VIPs, and also put on an athletic display in the gymnasium. The bad news was that this was going to involve weeks of marching and gymnastics practice so that things would be just right on the day. Over time it seemed that the focus upon the college opening ceremony was actually to the detriment of our studies as young Police Officers.

An early notification that didn't mean a lot to me and others at the time but came to grow in importance many years later was the following statement, "Thanks for joining guys. Just to let you know that we have a thing called superannuation and it's compulsory. That means that you won't be getting 6% of your salary (this was to grow to 7.5% when early retirement and the ability to medically disengage (PERF) was introduced a few years later). The good news is that the Government will put in double of your contributions and it will all get taxed a bit. It won't mean much to you guys now but you will thank us when you are old and grey." I certainly came to appreciate this later, as the best thing that the New Zealand Police ever did for me.

So, our training continued and it seemed that things would be alright on the day of the opening. Not for me though. The rugby trials were held a few days before the big event. As I got up from the first ruck of the day, I noticed a sizeable rectangular hole in my right knee. Very clean at first but then it started to fill with blood. I was taken off to Porirua Hospital for a few stitches. Over the next couple of days, it got infected and I was having trouble walking. It did recover to the extent that I was able to march at the opening ceremony with a slightly discernible limp. However, there was no way that I was able to take my part in the gymnastics display being relatively uncoordinated at the best of times. I recall not receiving a huge amount of sympathy from the PE staff but I've still got the scar to prove it.

Following the ceremony our Wing had lunch with Prince Charles in the massive college dining room. This was the first time that I had encountered royalty. He certainly seemed pleasant enough and appeared very interested and engaging. I recall him saying something to the effect that it was wonderful to open a complex that was actually new. I also noted that it was quite difficult to understand everything that he was saying. Clearly the English he spoke was different to that taught to me in South Auckland. I'm sure that other encounters with royalty will crop up from time to time.

I wrote about the opening of the College for our Wing yearbook. This is what my eighteen-year-old self had to say. He reluctantly waives copyright to his older, wiser self. If you feel like skipping this bit I understand because it is pretty bad:

THE OPENING OF THE NEW ZEALAND POLICE COLLEGE AT PAPAKOWHA, PORIRUA, 1 APRIL 1981

The day dawned bright and clear and those who had put the many hours of planning into what was hoped to be the New Zealand Police's proudest day breathed a sigh of relief.

Even at the early hour of 7 am the catering staff, under the direction of Sergeant Brown had been up for several hours preparing the hundreds of meals that had to be provided for the guests and interested parties. As the clock ticked over a couple more hours, final preparations were still going on; from the Cadet point of view this involved dusting of uniforms, eager polishing of already impressive shoes and of course, the calming of nerves before the great day ahead.

As the Cadets waited in the changing rooms of the magnificent new gymnasium, guests began to file in, eager to see the much talked about and practised gym routine that the P T staff and Cadets had in store. Before long, all seating room was taken leaving only standing room for those who were even a fraction late. News came through that His Royal Highness Prince Charles had been detained longer than expected at the Waitangirua Shopping Mall but that news served to make the crowd even more excited, as the sounds of the combined bands lofted in from the parade ground. Presently the Prince did arrive and directly on cue the display began. Twenty-seven and a quarter electrifying minutes later it was over but the rest of the proceedings were just beginning.

The Prince was escorted to the Crimes Scene House where a murder scene was being investigated under the control of Detective Inspector O'Donovan and Detective Senior Sergeant Moore.

Meanwhile, the Cadets, after a quick change from P T gear to parade uniform, were assembling with the combined bands, Sergeants' course and the Senior Constables, who along with the dogs and dog handlers- already on the parade ground performing an impressive display- were to form the official parade. The order "Parade Quick March" given by Parade Commander Inspector Jenner made everyone realise that there was no turning back now. However, the marching came naturally, a fitting tribute to the hours of practice put in with Senior Marley's voice of command ever present. The parade came to a halt as close as can reasonably be expected to the correct point.

The speeches then followed. Firstly, a speech of welcome by Commissioner Walton who expressed the pleasure felt by the whole of the New Zealand Police in the Prince's attendance at the opening ceremony. Then the Prime Minister spoke of the history of the New Zealand Police and also graced the Prince of Wales Cadet Wing with the words "a quality intake in a quality college, bearing an honoured name". The humour, wit and spontaneity displayed by the Prince in his speech probably surprise some of his audience who are not used to hearing royalty speak in such a down to earth approach. The Prince certainly won a great deal of admiration for his approachable manner. He then unveiled the commemorative plaque and declared the new Police

College open, commenting that it was nice to be actually opening something that was in fact new.

An unexpected thing then happened. The Prince asked to inspect the Prince of Wales Cadet Wing. A command of "Open Order" was heard and although the manoeuvre had not been properly practised it was executed with only slight tentativeness. Due to a lack of time the Prince inspected only the front row of each of the three sections, and left the parade ground hopefully suitably impressed with what he saw.

Next came lunch. A dinner of curry, rice, chicken chow mein, sweet and sour pork, deep fried fish, cold meats, and a selection of vegetables and salads. For those still hungry, there were gateaux, fruit salad and trifles for dessert. The Prince chose to dine with the Cadets of his Wing and all had a chance to speak with him. The range of topics that the Prince was able to relate to was truly amazing. At the completion of the meal a plaque was presented to the Prince by Peter Broughton on behalf of the Prince of Wales Cadet Wing.

So, all too soon the opening of the Police College and the visit of HRH Prince of Wales was just a memory, but I am sure that each of the Cadets and the staff of the College will remember the 1st of April 1981 for the rest of their lives." Enough said, I think.

After the opening, things started to settle down a bit as we progressed into learning what being a Police Officer was all about. The next out of classroom event was the community service phase held over a two-week period. We were randomly assigned two community placements to satisfy this part of the course. Some scored the big-ticket organisations such as the Fire Service, Prison Service and Lake Alice Mental Institution. One story came back from there about an inmate who was tanked up on enough tranquilizer to knock over a horse yet he would still run around all day with another inmate over his shoulders. Sadly, for them, those sorts of people just can't survive in the outside world without making a mess of things. My assignments were a little more sedate. My first placement was with a local rest home. The days there involved chatting with the residents, playing copious hands of cards (I'm not going to confirm whether strip poker was on the menu) and drinking tea continuously. One encounter though was to stick with me for the remainder of my career. One old dear spent her time making small items such as wallets and key pouches. On my final day she presented me with a dark green leather key pouch. After graduation I made the decision to use it to hold my handcuff and locker keys from that day forward. Every shift that I went to work in uniform for over 37 years that key pouch could be found in my right-hand trouser pocket. My benefactor is of course long deceased. The key pouch is now looking a little the worse for wear, a bit like me, I guess. In a way it is most certainly one of my prized possessions.

My second posting was to the Lower Hutt Social Welfare Office. I was assigned to a social worker who dealt with troubled youth. Even though I had grown up in South Auckland, parts of the Hutt Valley were quite an eye opener. The opportunity to visit Epuni Boys Home was quite sobering. It all culminated with being allowed the opportunity to view a sitting of the Lower Hutt Children and Young Persons Court which featured some of the youths that I had met earlier in the week. I was introduced to the Police Prosecutor and almost immediately I had the feeling that was something I might like to do at some stage. Watch this space, I guess.

Into July and we were all despatched to our home areas for station duty. The Otahuhu Police Station was just down the road from my father's house. The five weeks on station duty with assignments to staff on a variety of policing roles convinced me that I was on the right path to a rewarding career. Simmering in the background over this period but not overly significant at that point was the Springbok Rugby Tour of New Zealand and the potential for civil disorder. The tour commenced at Gisborne, and there was a reasonable amount of protest, but things appeared under control. The game against Waikato at Hamilton on the final weekend of our station duty was something completely different. Protestors were able to breach the lines of Police and security and a large number of them made it onto the pitch prior to the match. This then left an incredible situation of a few hundred protestors being surrounded and ultimately protected by Police from thousands of rugby fans angry that the match had been called off. This turn of events changed everything.

We had all returned to the Police College and it was apparent that Police hierarchy were turning on the heat. A newly arrived Recruit Wing suddenly became 'Green Squad' and our Wing were used as mock protestors for the training of Blue and White Squads. Thankfully Red Squad was being trained elsewhere. Much has been said of this highly trained group of officers. One of their Senior Sergeant's, Ross Meurant, wrote a really good account of the Springbok Tour called the Red Squad Story. It's well worth a read for more information. The next blow for sensibility and order was the Molesworth Street riot on the evening of Wednesday 29 July 1981. This street is significant as it houses the Beehive and Parliament as well as Police National Headquarters. The violence here was reportedly incredible in terms of New Zealand standards with both sides afforded some blame. Matters had clearly gotten out of hand. Serious steps were required to be taken. So, the powers that be determined that the sixty members of the Prince of Wales 25th Cadet Wing should be immediately sworn in and put to service. Thirty of us were sent to Auckland and accommodated at the YMCA, the others remained in Wellington. I'm fairly confident to say that this action was unprecedented in terms of the history of the New Zealand Police. There was a small ceremony to take care of the official business and we were advised not to get carried away with our change of status and pay rise of more than 500%. A lot of cops from that period will have many and varied Springbok Tour stories. Those are their stories to tell, far more exciting than mine I'm picking, but for a newly turned nineteen-year-old it was still quite an adventure.

Our mission was simply to provide cover so local cops could have a day off and to provide numbers at lower level protest activity. I was assigned to the Auckland Beat Section. The week revolved around a protest on Saturdays and on Wednesday evenings with normal policing taking care of the rest. It was a bonus to be instructed by some experienced Officers who were able to show the benefits of skulking around the city looking for those up to no good. A great example one evening was when I was directed to dive into an alcove between buildings by my partner, moments before a uniformed patrol car drove past. As it did, he threw a rock at the rear door of the Police vehicle causing quite a racket, which just drove on by completely oblivious to us in the shadows. I was saddened to learn a few years later that one of the Officers I had worked with, had himself been convicted of committing multiple burglaries whilst on duty. I'm told that a dog handler tracked the offender from an inner-city office to the Auckland Central Police Station one evening. The handler misread the situation and thought that his dog was pulling his leg and big growls were given. I wonder who had the last laugh. I can certainly attest that nothing untoward was noticed by me when I was working with this guy.

My first experience of protest action was a Wednesday march from Aotea Square to Eden Park. This was followed by a bit of chanting and then the return walk to Aotea Square. A pleasant enough stroll I guess, but my new shoes were starting to cause blisters and there was some idiot with a megaphone screaming directly at me for the entire time. If he had only asked nicely, I could have explained that I already had the chant committed to memory.

About two weeks out from the final test I was involved in what would come to be remembered as the "Battle of the Gateway Lodge". This old endearing airport environs hotel was to be where the Springboks were to be staying for the final part of the tour. A protest was planned in the vicinity on the Saturday afternoon of the Wellington test match. A few hundred protesters gathered near the intersection of Massey Road and George Bolt Drive. I was part of the one hundred or so Police Officers assigned to look after the event. The protesters commenced by marching down George Bolt Drive towards the Auckland International Airport in a fairly uniformed fashion. This obviously concerned the Police Operation Commander because he placed his entire resource a few hundred metres further down George Bolt Drive between the protestors and the airport. Having achieved their aim, the protestors reversed and began running back towards the Gateway Lodge. At that time only a skeleton crew of Officers were on site to protect the premises. We were quickly ordered to board a couple of buses and were off in pursuit. It was too dangerous to travel along George Bolt Drive because the straggling protestors were taking up the whole road, so we had to go the long way via Westney Road. We arrived just in time as the fastest of the protestors were arriving. As our bus ground to a halt the Senior Officer on board ordered not overly specifically, "Get in amongst them". Most of us didn't need a second invitation and it was quite an ugly scene for a few minutes. It was clearly a points victory for the tactics of the protest leaders, but we were able to regain order without any serious damage being caused.

Likely as a result of this incident a decision was made that the Springboks would be housed in temporary accommodation within the Eden Park complex. Just to make sure, the entire site was surrounded with jumbo bins and barbed wire enclosed the pitch. For the final two weeks of the tour I was on Night Shift security at Eden Park. Nothing really happened but someone had to do it. On the morning of the final test I was on duty at the front gate an hour or so before knock off. I noticed the Operation Commander approaching the gate with other senior police staff. I opened the gate in an efficient and timely manner before receiving a rebuke from the Operation Commander for not checking his identification. The fact that he was in full uniform and was also well known seemed to escape notice. Mental note- Police management can be pedantic at times. I was so tired that I didn't even get up until half time to watch the final test on television. By that time, all hell had broken loose for the staff on duty including the antics of Marx Jones letting fly with flour bombs from his Cessna aircraft on numerous bombing runs.

The events surrounding the Springbok Rugby tour of 1981 are now firmly set into New Zealand folk-lore with a number of books and movies recording the events. I was interested to see it as the backdrop to some episodes of the popular series Westside a couple of years back. When one of my sons showed me his New Zealand History homework, I felt some pride in having played a small part in this tumultuous event. I did feel the need to correct his teacher who was proclaiming that the leader of Red Squad was Ross Meurant, even though as previously mentioned, he did write the book. I was making my way into Eden Park in 1994, when contact had resumed between the All Blacks and the Springboks. I happened to run into retired Inspector Phil Keber, the actual Red Squad commander, and pointed out that it was quite a bit more orderly than when he was there in 1981. He was just pleased that he was going to get to see the rugby this time.

We returned to Police College after our unexpected additional station duty. There was a ceremony to signify our demotion back to Cadet and of course we reverted back to a fifth of the salary that we had enjoyed for our past five weeks service. The only change of status that came about from our efforts was that we were allowed into the Bar on Saturday afternoons for a couple of hours. Talk about a return to the six o'clock swill. The instructors were beginning to worry about the amount of classroom time that we had missed, although the practical experience obtained from the six weeks of Station Duty and five weeks of Springbok Tour duty away from college was invaluable. Still, it was certainly a period of getting back down into some hard work.

One of the things that slightly bothered me then and surfaces from time to time via social media, was a strange occurrence during our sports teams' photograph sessions. After the standard photographs were taken, we were asked to strip down to our underwear for an additional photograph. As I say, it seemed a bit strange to me but who was I to say no. I'm fairly certain that would not occur in this day and age. Whether the Department is liable for this or not, I suppose that it remains to be seen.

Most of the Wing had earlier committed to being part of the biennial sporting exchange with the Queensland Police Academy. In early November quite a group of us, many travelling overseas for the first time, boarded an Air New Zealand DC8 and headed for Sydney. Again, I failed to see the logic of this but we pulled up at our accommodation in Kings Cross and were told not to be late for the bus in two days' time. In hindsight I guess that this was another test as there was quite some potential to lose a Cadet or two during that stay. We then flew to Brisbane and met up with our Queensland counterparts. We were billeted for the first weekend. A colleague and I were in the back of a Holden Belmont being driven by my billet and his colleague was riding shotgun. They were trying to egg us on by suggesting that we were somehow racist because of the Springbok tour. Somewhat incredibly, a few minutes later on the passenger gave a spray of abuse out the window at a couple of Aboriginals as we passed. It seemed that they still had a lot to learn. We had a few days down at the Coolangatta Surf Club and got so sunburnt that playing football against the Queenslanders was quite uncomfortable. That's my excuse for the loss anyway.

Final exams beckoned upon our return to Porirua. I ended up third in my section of twenty but also third overall in the Wing. I'm guessing that because I would have topped either of the other sections, I was presented with the section "Progress Prize" for most improved. No sign of Prince Charles at the graduation; too busy I suppose being a newlywed and all. A reunion would have to wait for another time. Interestingly a decision was made that as we had missed so much classroom work, we would remain at the College for two weeks after graduation to 'catch up'. Another unprecedented event I imagine. Although it does make you wonder why we were taught the Police Offences Act 1927 when it was to be repealed as at 1 April 1982. The Summary Offences Act 1981 took its place and no one had the good sense to put it into the syllabus. That's the Police, I guess.

1   The Prince of Wales 25th Cadet Wing.

2 B Section, Prince of Wales 25th Cadet Wing.

3 Police College Opening Ceremony 1 April 1981.

4 The Parade awaiting inspection.

5 Yours truly at left rear of B Section.

6 "What a fine bunch of chaps, Commissioner. I think that I'll invite them over for tea one day"

2. LET'S GET THIS PARTY STARTED!

I was appointed to Section Three, Otahuhu from January 1982 as a General Duties Constable. It was immediately apparent that the section of a Senior Sergeant, two Sergeants and eighteen Constables were extremely experienced and hard working. They were tough and uncompromising but also very fair, generally playing to the rules (the criminals of course weren't). The next least experienced to Tracker and I as the newbies, had just completed two years, a life time in South Auckland terms. Yes, you read it correctly, Tracker and I had been assigned on Section together, who would have guessed? At that time centralisation was in vogue so all staff commenced duties from Otahuhu Station apart from the two-person Howick patrol. Over the years, reflecting different management practices, centralisation and decentralisation danced a merry tune. I took my turn in the rotation of duties being based at Mangere, Otara and Howick. If staffing allowed, the Papatoetoe and Manukau coverage was provided from Otahuhu. It occurred to me fairly early on that I looked young, because in fact I was. I was required to patrol licenced premises even though I was not yet old enough to enter them off duty. The answer was to join the crowd and grow a moustache. It's still here 37 years later with no real plans to shave it off any time soon.

Being mistaken for Tom Selleck from time to time is the least of my worries!

With General Duties came shift work. The rotating shifts in those days were set in stone so forward planning was very easy. The Five-Week roster commenced on a Saturday with seven Early Shifts (0700-1500). Two days off followed by seven Night Shifts starting on the Monday night (2300-0700). Starting Night Shift on a Monday night certainly gave the opportunity to work into the week so to speak. If the community behaved itself then things could proceed fairly civilly until Thursday night. This would then often lead to three busy, sometimes manic nights, hopefully followed by a quiet Sunday to clean up the paperwork. There is something to the saying that a full moon makes many people go crazy. A Night Shift with a full moon was always busier and often involved dealing with very strange people. Night Shift was followed by three days off then four Late Shifts commencing on Thursday (1500-2300). That was followed by a week of Twilight Shift commencing on the Monday. That week provided cover for the other four sections involved in the roster. You would be required to work four days of the seven and every opportunity was given for as many members as possible to be rostered for Training Day on the Wednesday. This enabled a brush up on new law and baton training and the like. If you were really unfortunate you could be rostered Twilight Shift from Thursday to Saturday (1900- 0300), and this basically was another period of Night Shift. The final week involved three Late Shifts from Monday to Wednesday (1500-2300), followed by two days off before it all started again. Generally, you weren't allowed to take Night Shift off unless you were taking off an entire five-week period. In short this gave you one weekend off in five or perhaps two if the Staff Senior Sergeant was able to roster a weekend off for you on the Twilight Week. For those of you who have struggled to follow this narrative of the Five- Week Roster please be assured that it is the simplest of all rosters out there to follow. Some of the more recently adopted rosters include differing shift lengths and often a progressive staircase of a couple of earlies, followed by two lates and then nights. By all accounts the new generation of roster is supposed to be easier on the body. I had to laugh at a media report around this time. We were trying to garner public sympathy for another pay round and the Woman's Weekly produced an article quoting comments from a police spouse's association from down the line. One woman pointed out that the Officers in their area had to do seven nights in a row, giving the impression that it was unique to them. As I recall it didn't do them or us any good. Shift work was certainly tough on the body, mind and soul. I really admired some of the older members who were still on the Five-Week Roster and loving it long after I had moved onto greener pastures. It could certainly be described as more suitable for young people. I still recall early on when I would finish up at 7.00 am if I was lucky, picking up a Fresh Up and a Moro on the way home. I would get into bed and set the radio to a fifteen-minute snooze. It would be quite rare for me to hear the 7.30 news. It was fair to say that my sleeping became progressively worse over the three separate blocks of shift work that I did over the next few years. So much so, that a visit to a sleep specialist was met with "Oh, not another Police Officer!"

As promised in the first chapter here is the record of the Section's haze on me so you can have a good laugh. You should be ashamed of yourself if you do. Anyway, I think that it was during my second week of Night Shift. I was beginning to get used to the role and thought that the guys and girls on the section were pretty good sorts. How wrong was I? A job came in about some sort of disorder going down at the Pah Road Cemetery (it's called the Manukau Memorial Gardens today). I must have been tired because I should have smelt a rat. My partner steeled himself and began to resemble something from a Marvel comic. I drove slowly into the cemetery for a couple of hundred metres. It's as dark as, and old gravestones on both sides - you get the picture? Next second my partner utters something and dives out of his door and starts running away across some graves. I got out of the car, not entirely sure what was going on. I couldn't see my partner and there was no sound other than a slight moan coming from my right. Well, I was ready to resign then and there, 'Thanks for having me, it was a blast, I think I'll go and study to be a lawyer now". My senses exploded when a couple of what could only be described as ghouls started chasing me. I'm surprised that I didn't have a heart attack (at nineteen unlikely, but I gave it a good go) or shit myself (or did I?). So that was a great laugh all round. I was beginning to learn that you needed a special sense of humour to have any chance of surviving as a Police Officer.

One haze that did occur on Section that I thought was funny occurred on a quiet Sunday Night Shift; it was always Night Shift. I went into a cold sweat just thinking about them. One of the guys on Section had a vehicle that was his pride and joy. He usually parked it at the Otahuhu Police Station in a nice spot under a security light. His mistake was that he always left his keys in his file tray when he was out on patrol. A couple of hours into the shift, the plan was put into action. The Watchhousekeeper grabbed the keys to his colleague's car and shifted it out of sight. The radio dispatcher was in on the gag so when one of the patrols reported that a vehicle was failing to stop for them a mock high-speed pursuit was underway. The pursuing patrol was able to get close enough to see the offending vehicle's registration number, which of course was the same as the targeted Officer's car. He wasn't having a bar of it and drove back to the station to console his pride and joy. His mood changed when the vehicle wasn't where he had parked it. The 'pursuit' was progressing well with about three units involved in trying to get it back for their beloved colleague. This went on for quite a while, but alas; the scrote driving it misjudged a corner and the car was smashed up so bad that it was probably beyond repair. The cop arrived at the 'scene' to find a host of cars with flashing blue lights and even a tow truck or two. Of course, his car was nowhere to be seen. Glory days!

Sometimes you just didn't know what you were going to encounter. One Night Shift, my partner and I were patrolling around the industrial area up off Harris Road, East Tamaki. That area is completely developed today but back in the 80's the roads were in place but there was quite a bit of bare land. As we drove down a cul de sac near Allen's Road, at the end, a few metres off the roadway, was a rather unusual sight. There was a group of about twenty people in bright white gowns and hats not wildly dissimilar to the KKK. They were dancing in a circular fashion around a small fire in the middle. Satisfied that there was no human sacrifice going on I thought to myself "There is no way we are going over there to find out what they are up to" ….and we didn't.

One morning our section turned up bright eyed and bushy tailed for an Early Shift. The muster room was a sight to behold. From floor to ceiling, it was literally covered in boxes of women's lingerie. It seemed that one of the Night Shift patrols caught a guy in East Tamaki doing a bit of discount shopping with a bit of a sexual overtone from his neighbour's clothesline. The patrol made the rookie mistake of asking this perp if he had any more at home. Deciding that it might be time to come clean, the Officers were told that there might be one or two more stolen knickers lying around at his house. Over the next few hours, boot load after boot load of lingerie found its way to the Otahuhu Police Station. Nearby there was a Bendon factory. It must have been working overtime to supply the market with replacements for the product this guy was purloining from clotheslines in the area. A few years later

I had occasion to visit this house when I was doing enquiry duties from Otara. I knocked on the door and was invited in. There was literally a small pathway along the hallway and then into each room. The remainder of the house was just a massive collection of junk. Suddenly I was being offered a coffee. "No thanks, I'm trying to give it up". "How about tea then?" "Ah, it gives me wind". "Do you want a biscuit?" I couldn't get out of there quick enough.

A couple of years in, I got taught quite a lesson by a young criminal. It was one of those bitterly cold (for Auckland anyway) nights, and it was pouring down from time to time. Great coats were a thing of the past and those lined duty jackets had yet to arrive. I had a jersey over the top of my shirt and my black raincoat over the top of that. Even though it was raining, you were still expected to get out of the car and talk to people. On that note I chuckle today when I see how illuminated the frontline staff are, day and night. How one of us didn't get bowled over when we were on the roads in our black rain coats I don't know. On this night we were driving along St George Street, Papatoetoe. We were about to stop a vehicle in front of us when it pulled over and two occupants got out and ran. My partner headed after the driver and the front seat passenger was mine. My guy headed down a driveway and into the backyard of a residential address. The fences were fairly high and sheer so I managed to catch up with him as he was trying to get over one. Initially he was fairly compliant and I had him assume the position against the fence. Out came my handcuffs and just as I was about to apply the first, he reached over and grabbed the upper back of my raincoat which began to ride up over my head seriously affecting my movement. Not a particularly good position to be in I might add. We started to have a bit of a scrap including a tug of war over my handcuffs. He got control of them and I took a couple of heavy blows to the head. I knew that I needed to get in close to minimise the damage. In reality, I was biding for time for my partner to arrive so that we could beat the shit out of this guy. However, I was soon to find out that this crim knew all the tricks. As we wrestled in close, I suddenly found myself with his hand down my throat trying to give me an amateur tonsillectomy. Now you would think that the obvious reaction to this was to bite down hard and see how many fingers I could sever. Wrong! My senses were screaming out for that piece of shit to get his hand out of my mouth in the most amazing of gag reflexes. By this stage I was bleeding so much that I couldn't really see. As most people know, head wounds bleed profusely even though the injury might not be that bad. I did have the odd thought that I might not make it out of this one and that I might not be around for the big super payday I was promised at the Police College. I was determined to stay on my feet as I knew that it was probably all over if I went down. The guy decided that he had better get out of there before backup arrived and that the boot might be on the other foot as it were. He went over a side fence taking my handcuffs with him and I staggered out the front. My partner was just down the road looking for me and another patrol was just arriving. I must have looked like I was on death's door so we headed off to Middlemore Hospital.

I was cleaned up and it wasn't too bad. I had three cuts to my head requiring something like fifteen stiches. My throat had taken a bit of a hammering and speech was a little difficult but nothing that time wouldn't heal. I know that some of you are thinking this, so I'll address the elephant in the room. Those whacks to the head might help explain a few things about me, there I've said it! The doctor told me to take a few days off. It might be alright for him but anyone who knows anything about frontline policing in South Auckland is aware that the Sunday night of Night Shift is when a lot of the arrest paperwork gets done. You didn't want those nasty Prosecutors getting all up in arms because they didn't have an arrest file. It had been a busy week and I had quite a bit of correspondence that just had to be done. I went in for line-up that night, my mistake being that I was in uniform. I looked like I had gone a few rounds with David Tua but I was assured by the Sergeant that I wouldn't be required on the street. Wrong! This was South Auckland after all, the section was short, and Control was screaming down the line demanding that the backlog of jobs get done. So, I was out there dealing to crime for the next four hours or so constantly having to tell members of the public that they should have seen the other guy! I finally got a chance to get into some of the paperwork but had lost so much time that a couple of hours of overtime were also needed.

That then left me with three rostered days off before I was back on duty again for the Thursday Late Shift. The end result was, that I took no sick leave for this incident. Knowing what I do now, if something similar had occurred to me at some time later, you wouldn't have seen me for months. The CIB did what they do best and apparently this guy couldn't resist telling what he had done to a mate who was friendly with the Feds. The Feds knocked over his house and lo and behold found my handcuffs. I was called in to do an ID even though I had said that the backyard was almost pitch black. It wouldn't have been admissible anyway because I was just shown the solitary guy in a holding room. I was invited to give him a bit of a tune up but dealing to someone in police custody is a little different to 'overcoming resistance' during an arrest.

The guy went to court and was charged, as you would imagine, with a serious assault. Initially he elected a jury trial and pleaded not guilty. That was okay by me because I knew what had happened even if it was a bit embarrassing. Communication wasn't particularly good in those days and at some stage I received word that the charge had been reduced and that he had pleaded guilty. Apparently, the fact that I hadn't needed any sick leave indicated to Crown Counsel that my injuries were superficial. I was tempted to offer to give one or more of them a few whacks around the head with a metal object to see how they liked it! In the end the shithead was sentenced to periodic detention. I know his name; his time might come.

When it was all over, I made enquiries to get my handcuffs back as they had been lodged as an exhibit. I was confronted with delay after delay and was finally told that the whereabouts of my handcuffs were unknown. Some bastard had stolen them, that's what happened! On the strength of this mysterious disappearance, I was able to requisition a replacement pair which duly arrived. They had obviously seen an arrest or two as they were an earlier model than those carried by my colleagues. Every time I would go to the annual defensive tactics training (and give them their yearly clean) the instructor would comment upon the age of them. I was able to be useful though, many years later when word was received at the Manukau Police Station, that a Senior Constable visiting a classroom in East Tamaki had been talked into handcuffing the teacher (don't read too much into this as I wasn't there). The cop had then realised that he couldn't find the key to remove them. His handcuffs were a similar vintage to mine, which were apparently quite rare, so I was able to assist in the release of the teacher, who fortunately could see the funny side of this. I was also subject to a strange occurrence when we got fitted for the Sabre stab resistant vests. The powers that be determined, that despite the cost, Prosecutors should be outfitted even if they were never likely to be worn. All the measurements were taken and a few weeks later mine arrived. To my surprise I found that one of my inserts already had a serrated cut in it and they were trying to recycle it on me! Wrong, I sent that puppy back demanding that if I get stabbed, I want to be stabbed through a new vest, thank you very much!

If your luck was in, then a concert or major sporting event would fall during your Twilight week. The section on Twilights was the easiest for the Staff Senior Sergeant to roster en masse for the special event. It was pretty much luck of the draw at these events as to which part of the venue you were assigned to, and of course that dictated how much of the event that you got to take in. I struck gold (or was it a Heart of Gold?) at a Neil Young concert at Western Springs, when a colleague and I were assigned to amble slowly backwards and forwards within the inner bowl. Clearly, we spooked someone at an early stage in proceedings because we stumbled upon a huge bag of loose cannabis. We had no idea how it had found its way into our path and I bet that the owner was rather annoyed as well, but counting their lucky stars. I was on duty for "The Police" concert at Western Springs in 1984. Not so much fortune with the assignment on this occasion. I was part of a section of five staff placed on Old Mill Road, Grey Lynn around from the top gate to provide perimeter security. Things began in a fairly orderly fashion. It was quite a line-up that night, with Bryan Adams and the Australian Crawl warming the crowd up. Our vantage point meant that we couldn't see anything, and the audio was fairly muffled at best. Our staffing level was likely assigned upon experience from previous concerts at the venue. Along Old Mill Road was a row of houses separated from the stadium by a fairly high iron fence. Stories abound about sprightly fans without tickets scaling this fence. I even recall one of my brothers telling a yarn on just this point from his teenage years. Apparently, it involved one of his friends breaking her arm on the way over but not being allowed to seek medical attention until after the show. None of this would compare with what was to occur on this evening. It must have been a very well planned and coordinated assault because just on dusk, literally hundreds of people stormed through a particular property (the owners may or may not have been in on the plan). This group then demonstrated the power of the people by pushing the entire fence over. It was built in such a way that when one panel went, it all did. The five of us on duty up there were pretty powerless to do anything. This was civil disobedience at its finest, and we had to accept that the interlopers had taken a knockout victory that day. It would be hard to estimate just how many ticketless patrons got in, but it was certainly sizeable in number. When the lights went on at the end of the show the level of damage was simply amazing. As a result of this incident a very solid, even more substantial concrete wall, was constructed around the upper environ of Western Springs and I understand that it is still in place pretty much unscathed today.

I had my second brush with royalty during the tour of Prince Charles and Princess Diana when they brought Prince William downunder in 1983. One day involved being tossed out of a Police bus on Hurstmere Road in Takapuna to keep the crowd at bay for a few minutes until the royal motorcade had passed. We were then off to Manukau City Centre where the Fire Service put on a display for the royals. I recall that a toy fire engine, and possibly a buzzy bee was presented for Prince William. I was also on duty when the royal couple attended a gala performance at the St James Theatre in Queen Street. The word was that there wasn't to be a large Police presence during the show. All we did for that shift was to get into position outside the theatre when the couple arrived, then head back to Central for a couple of hours of violent videos and then head back down for the departure. There was a media report at one stage about Police watching violent videos during down time. Surely, they weren't suggesting that we watch Bambi? Despite my attendance there was no motivation from Prince Charles for a reunion. Perhaps he just didn't see me in the crowd. It looked like it may have to wait for a later time.

During the early days on Section I had my first experiences with the Judicial System. The Otahuhu District Court was a pretty busy place, probably only bettered by the Auckland District Court, although Christchurch always seemed to manipulate statistics to put themselves into second place. The long-standing system in place in New Zealand is that Police charge people who they have good cause to suspect have committed an offence. That may involve an arrest or the issue of a summons to appear in court. The Courts have a role to determine the validity of the process having regard to statute and case law. The referee if you will. The defendant, being the person who is charged, is assisted towards legal representation if it cannot be afforded. The Court then expects that the defendant pleads either guilty or not guilty. Generally, before or after a review of the evidence, the overwhelming percentage of defendants plead guilty. As we have all said from time to time, the Police are far too busy to lock up innocent people! That leaves about 20% or so of cases in which the defendant maintains a not guilty plea. In the early days there was no further examination of those cases before a defended hearing was scheduled. This would involve the witnesses from both sides attending court to give their evidence before the Judge, who would determine whether each charge had been proven beyond a reasonable doubt. In more modern times, more effort has been put in place to attempt to resolve cases short of a trial. This saw the advent of case management meetings and case review hearings. It was and probably still is the situation, that around 10% of apprehensions by an Officer require an attendance in court. I was vocal from time to time around this point, as it was my belief that the Police Administration should acknowledge this, and build this expectation into staffing levels. They didn't see it that way, and it was not uncommon for Officers to attend court on Days Off, Night Shifts and before Late Shifts. It's just one of those things really and will probably always be the same.

A couple of my early cases enabled me to form the opinion that some Judges had come from quite sheltered backgrounds and were lacking real world experience. It was also apparent to me that sometimes the facts didn't really matter and that a decision was given because it felt right. I'm not really complaining too bitterly because the District Court could probably best be described as a "court of the people". One example involved a fairly stock standard shoplifting from a local supermarket. The defendant was probably in his sixties and accepted stealing the item but gave no explanation. I recall that he had some criminal history, but I wouldn't describe him as a hardened criminal. I was somewhat surprised when I was advised that he had pleaded not guilty and I attended court on the appointed date. I knew that things were going to get a bit awkward when I noticed the defendant in the foyer of the court. He was wearing a somewhat tired black suit, but his chest was resplendent with war medals. I'm guessing Korea or Vietnam rather than WWII but it looked fairly impressive. When the case was called the Judge took one look at the defendant and then gave me the evilest glare. I tried to give my evidence, but it was extremely apparent that I was the person on trial. Not surprisingly the Judge found a technical issue that enabled him to dismiss the charge. The defendant walked free; the public gallery glared at me with disdain. I just hope that the medals were the defendant's and that he hadn't borrowed or worse still, stolen them!

I attended court a few weeks later in relation to a great catch that we had made in the Otara Town Centre carpark. A report had come in of a guy who was trying to break into vehicles. We cruised on in, parked up and went in on foot. We apprehended this guy with a bunch of what looked like locker keys. He had one of them in the driver's door external lock. When apprehended he also had a length of nylon packing tape in his pocket. Again, I was surprised when a not guilty plea was entered. It was clear to me when I was giving evidence that the Judge was having some trouble getting the point. He kept repeating to me "But these are locker keys, not car keys". Anyone with half a brain would know that anything sharp stuck into a 60s or 70s vehicle lock had a pretty good chance of opening it. He said, "What's all this, with this piece of nylon tape?" I explained that it could be folded over and squeezed between the door pillar and the door itself. Cars in those days usually had protruding door knobs which could be popped with the nylon tape. I even told the Judge that Police Officers carried some around the band of our forage caps to get into a car if needed. I didn't have the heart to tell the Judge that you could also get into Holden Kingswoods and some other vehicles using a standard black comb. This was all too much for the Judge and it was time to chalk up another loss for the good guys. It was clear to me that at the right time I was going to have to become a Prosecutor to try to even up the ledger.

This is probably a good time to spin another yarn, almost on point. One Sunday afternoon I was on patrol in the Mangere area with a female colleague. Now, I make mention of her gender here, not with any chauvinistic intent or to cast any aspersions. It is simply a fact, she was female. Again, it is a fact that has nothing to do with gender, that during that shift, the silly bitch locked the keys in the patrol car, on two separate occasions. The first time around, I was able to do the decent with the nylon tape that I had secured in the band of my forage cap. Feeling pretty pleased with myself, I recall looking around to see if there were any District Court Judges about, who might marvel at my handywork. The second occasion was about an hour after the first. This time we were parked behind a diary in Mangere Central. Try as I might, the old nylon tape just didn't want to work this time. To make matters worse, we had received notification on our portable radio, that our attendance was required reasonably urgently elsewhere in our patch. Neither of us felt inclined to fess up to our dispatcher about the predicament that we were in. A serious entry in the Jug Book was probably the start of our worries. A couple of nosey children aged about ten approached us. They quickly summed up the situation and made a proposal. We immediately agreed to their conditions, which involved us turning our backs while they took less than a minute to gain entry to the vehicle…this was Mangere after all. I guess that we were fortunate that they didn't flog the car, once they got it open. The fee was an ice block each, which I have to say was pretty reasonable in the circumstances. Before long we were on our way and the rest of our Section were none the wiser. This can't be the end of this matter though, surely a larger ethical dilemma exists here. As a result of our tacit agreement to benefit from, and indeed encourage their obvious criminal talents, are we somehow responsible for any future victims and also the cost of any likely incarcerations? Who really cares! We avoided entry into the Jug Book after all. More on the Jug Book later.

One time I was at court and I chuckled at what I saw. A detective was also at court waiting to give evidence. I didn't really know him but he was adjusting and fiddling with his tie far too often for my liking. I looked up at the Judge, who you guessed it, was wearing the same tie. I later learnt that it was the school tie for a prestigious Auckland high school. I thought the whole thing was strange. Of course, it was probably just a coincidence as I didn't believe that there was such a thing as the old boy network at play around here. Perhaps I was just naïve again. Many years later when eminent lawyer Mina Wharepouri was appointed to the District Court bench I was tempted to dig out my old school tie and try out this lark for myself. Kia Tamatane, brother.

There was a very strange occurrence one day when I was at court waiting for a case. All the defended hearings had been called in the List Court and about ten Officers and I were waiting for another courtroom to come free. A defendant was called up to be sentenced whilst we waited. He entered the dock and an elderly Escort Officer stood alongside him. The defendant was dressed immaculately in a full suit. As the Judge began the sentencing, things started to get quite weird. It became fairly clear that the defendant was going to be sentenced to imprisonment. Firstly, he removed his jacket and placed it over the dock. He then took off his spectacles and placed them on the ledge. He then loosened and removed his tie. This was followed by his watch and wedding ring. The Escort Officer appeared oblivious to this. About this time, the sentence was pronounced, and the defendant 'king hit' the Escort Officer who collapsed to the deck. All hell broke loose as the ten cops and I sprang forward from the back of the court to exact vengeance upon this defendant. Fortunately, there was not a huge response from the public so we were able to bundle this guy back to the cells. The Escort Officer was in a bad way and from my recollection that was the final act of his long career. The defendant was presented to the court again that afternoon and had another couple of years added to his sentence.

I once got charged with Careless Use of a Motor Vehicle. It's fair to say that I was an inexperienced driver when I joined the Police. Training at the Police College amounted to reversing around some cones on the parade ground, driving through the streets of Wellington and a hair-raising journey from Masterton to Upper Hutt over the Rimutakas. I say hair raising because we were told to drive as fast as we could! I thought that was pretty stupid but that's what institutionalism does to you. Anyway, after joining section it became a steep learning curve coming to grips with blue lighting all over South Auckland. It was only blue lighting in those days, as legend has it that a senior manager from parts north had been caught using his siren to get home to a scrumptious dinner and they were taken from the Police for a number of years. On this shift a high priority job was despatched to us. I flicked on the blue lights and cut down the Middlemore Hospital Access Road. I had to slow down going through there as it would be difficult to explain bowling over a person on crutches or in a wheel- chair. I then approached the S bends leading onto Swaffield Road Papatoetoe. The road was wet from recent drizzle, but the weather had been good for a couple of weeks or so. Someone speculated that there might have been some patches of oil on the road. As I went to exit the S bends the rear end of the Ford Falcon slipped away and I was unable to correct it and I took out a lamp post. I was driving so therefore it was my fault. I was just grateful that my patrol partner was not injured. Nursing a little bit of bruised pride, I then had the task of completing my first "TY367 Departmental Motor Vehicle Crash Form". I'm picking that form is familiar to some of you who are reading this. A decision was made by the powers that be that I should be charged with careless use of a motor vehicle. That wasn't a huge surprise to me. I expected that I would get a modest fine, probably not be disqualified and that there should be no impact on my employment. Hell, in those days' cops were able to survive drink drive convictions. What I was surprised by though, was the hour or so my Sergeant spent typing up the Information (the charging document) with my name on it with apparent glee. Up to that point I thought that he was quite a decent guy. To his credit though I saw him giving evidence in court a couple of times and it was a joy to behold. His tone, pace, manner of delivery had everyone eating from his hand. I'm not embarrassed to say that he could probably charm the knickers off a nun.

As this was an on-duty incident the Police Association provided a lawyer for me. As it panned out there was not a lot for the lawyer to do and I didn't even get to make an appearance in court. On Section there was a very experienced Constable who was also a very handy rally driver. This incident played on his mind and I'm guessing that he might have had the odd scare in one of those Ford Falcons, but had the skill to avoid disaster. I'm not able to state with certainty what the issue was but it had something to do with Limited Slip Diff and the light rear end on this particular model of vehicle. He was able to show mathematically that an 80 kg sand bag was needed in the boot of the vehicle for it to be stable under speed. The Department saw the error of its ways and withdrew the charge against me. I naively thought that there was more to this, so I arranged a meeting with some bloke at the Ford plant in Wiri. I was keen to point out these findings to him and was seeking that something be done about their unsafe vehicle. I must say that I got no traction at all from that meeting and I learnt that is not the way to settle multi-million-dollar law suits.

Despite the amount of high-speed driving going on, crashes were actually fairly rare. I did feel some sympathy for a colleague of mine who was involved in quite a spectacular crash. This Officer was a very good driver and to me anyway, he certainly gave the impression of knowing what he was doing. In the early hours of a Night Shift morning he and his patrol partner were in the Papatoetoe area. The night was fine and the roads were dry. A few minutes earlier they had passed through the intersection of Great South Road and Kolmar Road. A job came in that required them to blue light over to Otara. The Officer was heading along Kolmar Road towards Great South, probably quite quick. Those of you who have never been in such places around 3am won't know that the Great South Road amongst roads are serviced nightly by a cleaning truck that gives the roadway a nice wash for it to look good for the day shift workers. As the Officer approached the intersection, he realised too late that the truck has just been through and that the previously dry road was now under about two inches of water. The brakes were applied but the vehicle only wanted to travel straight and certainly didn't want to slow down. The patrol car ploughed straight through the front window of a real estate agency, coming to rest partway into the building. If that wasn't bad enough some smart alec thought that it would be funny to take and circulate a photograph of the scene with the police vehicle under a sign that read "Parking at Rear".

After work on our first Early Shift Wednesday, which also happened to be payday, Tracker and I were indoctrinated into the wonders of the jug session. As we had only been around for a few days neither of us had incurred the wrath of the jug master. Those who had, found their names in the Jug Book with a brief or sometimes grandiose explanation of the indiscretion. The jug session took place in the Otahuhu Police Club on the top level of the station. The Otahuhu Police Station of that era was very similar in design to many others around the country. On the ground level was the public counter, Watchhouse and cell area, muster room and offices for specialist groups. The first level had a meeting room and offices for other specialist and administration staff. The top level had some offices but was largely a bar area that was also used for the largest of station meetings. After the initial gathering and the holding of the Jug Session at the bar, it was then decided that takeaways would be consumed before a regroup at one of the senior member's home in Mangere Bridge. It was all going well for Tracker and I, until about midnight when we tried to make tracks. We after all, were still on Early Shift and fall in at the muster room was at 6.45am. Despite our best efforts neither of us could make a break for it. The word "kidnap" does spring to mind, but it was all good fun I suppose. Around 3 am Tracker and I managed to escape via a bedroom window whilst the remainder of the section was otherwise engaged. That left a couple of hours of rest before turning up for work. I swear that quite a number of the crew came in straight from Mangere Bridge. We were both wondering whether we would have the right stuff to keep up with the pace of this.

One of the things about being in a large station is the amount of staff turnover. Police certainly offer a variety of career paths with both specialist and management opportunities. So much so, that after three years Section Three bore very little resemblance to the one Tracker and I had originally been posted to. Within a year or so you were in charge of an incident patrol and responsible for the training and guidance of more junior staff. After three years I was looking forward to a change and I applied to join the Enquiry Office. A few years later Tracker and I would meet again as Sergeants on the same shift, when he was based at Mangere, and I was at Howick.

3. A CHANGE OF PACE.

My first shift in the Enquiry Office lasted four days. History records that it was Monday 18 February 1985. I arrived at Albion Road for the 8 am start. A couple of files were thrown my way to get me into the swing of things. I hadn't even gotten to the first coffee break when the Senior Sergeant said "you had better go home and get back quick with enough clothes for a few days". Unbeknownst to me, the evening before the Tutumangao Stream, on the lower slopes of Mount Te Aroha burst its banks and careered through a house causing three deaths and destroying quite a bit of the town of Te Aroha. The ongoing concern was that the natural water reservoir high above the town may give way under the pressure and cause more damage and potentially loss of life. By lunchtime, a group of about eight of us from South Auckland were surveying the damage. We were on ten-hour Late Shifts for the next three days whilst staying at the Morrinsville Hotel. As the town of Te Aroha had been evacuated, our job was to prevent looting whilst efforts were underway to stabilise the reservoir so that the clean-up could begin. The town was eerily quiet and I vividly remember being placed on a static point and being told "If the siren sounds you will have thirty seconds to get out of the way before the water arrives, so run like hell…and good luck!" Suffice to say, the crisis was averted in a couple of days and we arrived back in Auckland to finish our shift. My stay in the Enquiry Office at Otahuhu was quite brief before I was assigned to a permanent position at the Otara Patrol Base.

It was at Otara that I first encountered Colin and Eardley who, along with Laurie would become such great colleagues and friends during the Prosecutions phase of my career. I certainly had some great times on Enquiry duties at Otara. The first couple of months were fairly tough though. There were three Enquiry Officers who worked on a rotating Late Shift/ Early Shift roster. This gave one weekend off in three. Also, one week in three was the designated "receiving week". That is, any files deemed worthy of further enquiry by the Sergeant were assigned with the expectation that most would be completed within the three-week period, before it all started again. The problem was that the Officer who I took over from, had left things in a bit of a mess. There was something like fifty unactioned files when I took over, just as I was about to hit my own receiving week. It was a big learning curve but with some hard work I was able to get things under control after a few rotations. Uniformed Enquiry Officers tended to deal with matters that were important to the public even though some of it wasn't overly serious. People like to think that their house is secure, their car is safe and that their washing stays on the clothesline if they leave it out at night.

A long-term Sergeant had a car that was, to be polite, a little past its best. On occasions though, it was an excellent vehicle to use for some of our unofficial undercover stings that we got involved in. The grass growing out from the wipers really set the vehicle off nicely. Quite a few arrests could be put down to that vehicle rather than the somewhat more obvious white and blue Departmental issue. I had a huge amount of fun and gained a lot of experience dealing with a myriad of situations. Most were from the mid-range of seriousness downwards and of course nothing like the cases dealt with by the CIB. I had already determined that the commitment and energy required to survive in the CIB was something that I simply couldn't give.

Some criminals are truly brazen. I attended the scene of a house burglary at the end of a cul-de-sac in Otara. The point of entry/exit was a rear window. Right alongside the window was an orange tree in season. It was apparent that there was a trail of orange peelings to the front of the yard and then straight down the cul-de-sac. It veered into the driveway of a house that I knew to be the home of some bad young offenders. They had been schooled well and a cough was unlikely. I was pretty keen that I had enough for a search warrant and a friendly JP agreed. These guys were one step ahead of me though and had already fenced the stolen property, with denials all round. The moment of truth arrived when, even I had to accept that it was not likely that a Judge would see it my way with the orange peel trail, no matter how well I sold it. A dog track or fingerprints maybe, but I just had to sheet it home to experience. I just hope that these crims learnt to be a bit tidier from then on.

I was assigned another case which had been causing the Manukau Polytechnic some concern. Cash and other valuables were going missing from lecturers' offices after hours. It was suspected that cleaners were involved but there was no evidence to confront anyone with. CCTV didn't exist so I had to confront the situation head on. With the permission of staff, I became a tutor for a couple of evenings, dressed appropriately of course. I positioned myself in an office that was directly across the hallway from another one. I slipped a five dollar note partway under a book in the adjoining office and took a seat and waited. Some may call this entrapment but sometimes you just had to do what you had to. It could easily be argued that in a perfect world that five-dollar note should be safe from interference much the same as a bicycle or vehicle in the carpark should be. This situation suited me fine because I was studying for promotion exams at the time and this was a perfect opportunity to get in some study during work time. A while later a cleaner entered the target office and left a few minutes later. As I was apparently working late, there was a glance into my office but no attempt to do any cleaning. I quickly inspected the other office, and as I suspected the five-dollar note was missing. As it was mine and I didn't really want to lose it, I made contact with the cleaning supervisor who was completely onboard for fear of losing the contract. An approach was made to the suspect who immediately coughed and took me to her locker which contained quite a bit of other stolen property. Not too shabby, even if I do say so myself.

One day a young guy took a large knife to the Otara Town Centre seeking vengeance for some indiscretion. I was called over to support the initial crew who had him cornered near the library. This situation certainly highlights the evolving realisation that Police Officers were woefully lacking in protective equipment and tactical options in those days. The five of us in attendance were in shirts. No stab resistant vests for us. A dog unit wasn't available so our tactical options ranged from hands to batons. The plan, that was ultimately successful on this occasion was one of distraction and then to overpower the suspect. Very risky, but it was all that we had, short of a firearm and that probably was never going to happen. The advent of stab resistant vests, O/C spray and Tasers has certainly provided better and safer options to deal with violent offenders. I get really annoyed when do-gooders prattle on about the minute risks associated with spray and tasers. Certainly, safer than a bullet to the head I would have thought.

In 1986 the Physical Competency Test (better known as the PCT) became compulsory. Prior to that time there was an emphasis upon physical fitness in preselection testing and at Police College only. Nothing else was required after completing a fitness test as part of the permanent appointment process two years after graduation. New Zealand Police had come to the realisation that some of the banter about cops and donuts might be close to the truth. The trade-off was some extra days off to train and a bonus payment after each two-year compulsory assessment. The Police Association had no great concern as it was difficult to argue against something that was ultimately beneficial to the health and wellbeing of its members. Interestingly, I understand that some Australian forces are still hampered in following New Zealand's lead due to their unions taking a converse view. For those of you who haven't had the pleasure, the PCT is a practical fitness test designed to include certain activities that might occur in day-to day-policing. It commences with a short trailer push and the return of a wheel contained within. That's followed by a 200-metre run to a right-angled balance beam. Over that and a long jump, some zigzagging through cones, over a hurdle and under some others. Through a window frame and then over a solid wall. A short run to an 85kg mannequin which is dragged for 7.5 metres and then up and over a wire fence and a sprint to the finish. Pass times are defined by age and gender. Anything under two minutes is a very good time. The record is around 1 minute 30 seconds. On one occasion that I checked in for testing, the course was set up at Mount Richmond Domain, Otahuhu. At the time I was doing quite a bit of distance running for an upcoming marathon. What I am to describe illustrates the difference between good slow fibre fitness, required for a marathon and fast fibre fitness required to complete the PCT. I ran the 12 kilometres from my home in Manukau to Otahuhu and then took my turn on the test. At that time the solid wall was 6 foot 6 inches tall. On this day that wall was unfortunately a bridge too far for me and I just couldn't get over it. Through frustration and quite a bit of embarrassment I kicked the shit out of the wall a few times, much to the amusement of those attending before running the 12 kilometres home. My redemption would have to wait another week when I decided to drive to the venue this time. It wasn't just me who had difficulty on occasions with the wall. A Wellington police woman took the Department to the High Court successfully arguing that it was unlawful for residential fences to be higher than six feet. As a result of her efforts all of the PCT walls had six inches chopped off them. That certainly helped me until I was into my fifties, when the rules allowed me to touch the wall rather than going over it.

A considerable amount of time was spent chasing after young offenders. Luckily for me the Children and Young Person's Act 1974 was still the law of the day. The minefield that was to be created by the Children and Young Person's and Their Families Act 1989 was still quite a way off. A file would arrive where one offender had been apprehended for a burglary or the unlawful taking of a motor vehicle, and they named other offenders in their statement. It was my job to follow up with the other suspects. The most extensive one I received was when one offender named seven others who had been in the stolen car with him. In law, the word of one offender is generally only admissible against themselves but it gave you something to work with. Under the law as it stood, I was able to turn up at a house and greet the parents. I would explain that I was there to talk to Johnny about a stolen car. If I was lucky Johnny would get a quick clip round the ears, most often from Mum to soften him up, and then the notebook would come out and I'd record the confession. It was accountability for actions at its best. On a good evening I could do about five or six of these, and then spend the Early Shift the next day doing the paperwork referral to Youth Aid. That sort of efficiency is just not possible anymore after the New Zealand Bill of Rights Act 1990 came in to join forces with the CYP & F

Act 1989. Young offenders on the way up have now been given an incentive to get away with anti-social behaviour.

One of the duties of an Enquiry Officer was to attend and investigate any fatal crashes that occurred during your shift. This type of work can be very harrowing but perversely quite rewarding. One fatal crash occurred on Otara Road at mid-evening during winter. A vehicle full of gang members ploughed into the rear of a truck and trailer unit that was legally parked on the side of the road. The truck was well lit, and laden with wool bales so it was fairly heavy. When I arrived, it was apparent that at least two gang members were deceased and three others seriously injured. Word had quickly spread and other gang members had begun to arrive. It appeared as though their plan was to exact revenge upon the owner of the truck. This situation was beginning to turn very ugly, quite quickly. Fortunately, I spied a gang member who I had dealt with on a number of occasions. Most importantly, I had treated him reasonably and fairly. I thought that I had some influence over him. There were a couple of Police Officers present but I had to act promptly and assertively. I turned to this gang member and using the loudest and deepest voice I could, I yelled "You, sort out your boys and get them under control or all hell is going to break loose!" I still don't know what or where this hell I was going to unleash was going to come from, but it seemed to work and some semblance of order was restored to this difficult situation.

Sometimes you just had to call it as you saw it. One fine day, I was over at the Otara Town Centre doing my best impersonation of Community Policing by chilling out with the retailers and patrons. I heard a commotion over by Farmers. In those days there were still some nationally branded stores and it was still to be a couple of years before the name "Otara Chopping Centre" came into existence. This unfortunate title stuck after the brutal killing of 21-year-old David Fuko with a machete in May 1988. I spied a guy in his late 20's wearing trousers, a shirt and tie. He was somewhat out of breath but he was doing his best to catch a younger male in street-wear. This younger guy appeared to be having a whale of a time, almost tempting the other man to get closer. That is until I arrived on the scene. The young guy was like a possum in the headlights when I caught him on the chin with a beautiful stiff-arm tackle. If it was league it would have been called marginal, in rugby I would have been spending ten minutes in the bin, and had an appointment with the judiciary. As the young guy was prone on the deck the other guy, between gasps, was able to tell me that I had caught myself a recidivist shoplifter. Good on me! If I had called that one differently it probably would have been the end of my time in the job.

During my stint at Otara, decentralisation came back into vogue and a brand spanking-new Police Station was being constructed around the existing patrol base, which we were still occupying. Part way through, a large portion of the new building was burnt down in an arson attack one night. Our Sergeant, who was usually a calm, quietly spoken man, was livid. He appeared on national television staring down the screen like a crazed cross between Clint

Eastwood, Sly Stallone and Arnie Schwarzenegger. He was just daring the scumbags to have another go, which was likely to be over his dead body. It was a joy to behold and truly inspirational to staff far and wide. Thankfully the community let the station be completed and there was no need to start a war.

This Sergeant also came to the party, as it were, regarding my stag do in January 1986. A gathering had been arranged for a few beers to be put on at my Dad's place in Otahuhu for a few of my nearest and dearest. Unbeknown to me, my Dad made contact with my Sergeant and arrangements were put in place to create a bit of havoc. I was about four or five beers into the evening and I caught a flash of blue out of the corner of my eye. Before I could work out what was happening and high tale it out of there, the Otahuhu Team Policing Unit in full riot gear had marched into the back yard. Next minute I'm under arrest, Christ knows what for, and I'm being stepped back to the paddy wagon. We had to walk past Dad's swimming pool, unfenced of course, as they were in those days. How I, or anyone else didn't end up in it I still don't know. The neighbours were all out to gawk at the spectacle although such things were not entirely unknown in these parts. I was thrown into the back of the paddy wagon, none too ceremoniously I might add. Fortunately, it was still too early for any other miscreants to be in there with me. After the short drive back to the Otahuhu Police Station I could sense that the vehicle was being reversed into the wash bay. The doors were flung open and I copped a high-pressure hose in the chops. Just as well I was getting married in summer. After a couple of minutes dousing, I was pretty much sober, and I was told that I could walk home. These guys were fairly proficient at this carry on, and I wondered if it was perhaps a regular occurrence. More bracing than a court appearance for some, I'm sure.

Enquiry Officers were rostered from time to time on special duties as required. My third brush with royalty occurred on one such occasion in 1986. HM Queen Elizabeth II was in New Zealand as part of her Diamond Jubilee tour. This tour saw the advent of the walkabout. I had been directed to stand right outside the Civic Theatre on Queen Street, Auckland City. There was quite a turnout of public and I was constantly scanning the crowd as the Queen approached from Aotea Square. Next minute the Queen was right alongside me talking to her subjects and receiving gifts. I couldn't help thinking, where were her security detail, because I seemed to be pretty much on my own? It seemed that she had just wandered off a bit catching some of the others off guard. As it transpired nothing untoward happened and I wasn't required to do anything that may have earnt me a medal. I did note that when the Queen was alongside me, she didn't convey any message of good-will from Prince Charles. I wanted to tell her that I was still hanging out for the reunion.

On one occasion I turned up to work to be advised that I was required to head out to the airport. It was October 1986 and the Indian Prime Minister Rajiv Ghandi was visiting New Zealand. I met up with another Constable at a caravan that was alongside an Air India 747 aircraft parked at the eastern end of the airport. Our instructions were to follow that plane wherever it went. I'm not entirely sure what we were supposed to do if it actually took off. Most of the shift we were tucked up in the caravan, catching up on some women's magazines, although there were a couple of Indian security personnel around so we also chewed the fat with them. One interesting thing that we were told, so it must be true, was about the level of security surrounding the Prime Minister. We were advised that because the aircraft had been sitting around for a while, that it was not allowed to fly until every seat and fitting had been unbolted, searched and reattached. Not surprising in hindsight considering that Mr Ghandi was assassinated a few years later by a suicide bomber, who was part of his security detail. The word came mid-afternoon that the aircraft was going to taxi down to the main international gates to be ready for departure that evening. True to our instructions my colleague and I followed the 747 on its journey along the taxi way in our patrol car with lights flashing and all. I suppose our assignment was successful because the aircraft was not stolen or interfered with at any stage.

One Late Shift I was directed out to the airport again. Through the security checkpoint and onto the tarmac I ended up parking the patrol car alongside an Air New Zealand 747 aircraft that was attached to the departure gate. There were quite a number of Officers' present but we weren't being told too much. Eventually we learnt that it had something to do though with a threat relating to a piece of baggage that was to be loaded onto the aircraft bound for Los Angeles. All of the passengers were secured in a departure lounge and it seemed that there was to be quite a delay. By my count there were thirteen patrol cars on the tarmac alongside the plane, all with lights flashing, which suggests that we weren't really being told the full story. At one point a Qantas 747 aircraft arrived. As it taxied to a halt all that could be seen was startled passengers peering out the windows and wondering just what had happened to little old New Zealand. Shortly afterwards, and without any satisfactory explanation being given, the emergency was over and it was time to head back to base. Much ado about nothing really, I'm picking that it didn't even make the papers, however it was quite dramatic at the time. Someone must know the full story.

During my time at Otara I sat and passed the Police Sergeant's Promotion Examinations. At that time, it involved four topics, namely Statutes, Evidence, Administration and P & D (Practice and Duties). After passing the examinations and having completed at least five years' service you were able to apply for promotional vacancies. None of the rigmarole of the appointment process required these days (more about that to come!). At this time, promotion was on the basis of seniority. Seniority as opposed to service commenced upon being sworn in.

As a Cadet we were sworn in as members of the New Zealand Police after graduation (the fact that we had been sworn in and then unsworn during the year didn't seem to count). Collar numbers were issued in terms of the place obtained on the course. I came in third so my collar number was '7540'. The top-ranking Cadet was '7538'. If

I had spent more time studying and less writing non sensical articles for the Wing year-book I might have come first! Our beef was that Recruits were sworn in at the commencement of their course which meant that around 120 collar numbers (lower than ours) were reserved for the two Recruit Wings that started after us. A small point but important.

When I came to apply for a Sergeant's position in 1987, I was the most junior member on the list for the entire country. I was fortunate however that there were vacancies at Auckland, Otahuhu and Papakura advertised and to be determined at the same time. I applied for all three. Most others only applied for their preferred location. I was told on good authority that after the Auckland and Otahuhu vacancies had been completed the selection panel ran its fingers down the page looking to fill the final of three vacancies at Papakura. That in itself was fairly unusual for the size of the station. Their fingers came to rest at the final name on the list, and the only remaining applicant, which happened to be me. I was off to Papakura!

4. WHAT DO WE DO NOW SARGE?

I packed up my shiny bright Sergeant's stripes and headed off to Papakura. For a while at least I was to be the youngest NCO in the country. I wasn't overly familiar with Papakura. I had been down to McLennan Park a few times to play soccer as a kid but that was about it.

I was soon to learn that Papakura was quite a special place to work. The station was staffed by some truly amazing and talented people. While it's not my place to write the biography detailing the contributions made by some of the people who worked that area, I just hope that someone does. I was assigned to Section One. Papakura also worked the five-week roster and it was interesting that two other newly promoted Sergeants were appointed to a couple of the other sections at the same time. My section had six Constables aged between 22 and 25 years. I was 25 at the time so youth was certainly on our side. When I arrived four of the Constables had permanent appointment, which meant that they had at least two years' service and had passed the in-service training modules. The other two Constables were still studying. One of the Constables I inherited, later became a Deputy Commissioner. The basic shift pattern was to provide two Constables for the Papakura Incident patrol, two for the Manurewa Incident Patrol and a Watchhousekeeper to take care of the small cellblock and public counter. That allowed for one member to be on leave at any one time. Illnesses were rare but they could be problematic. If staff shortages were signalled in advance, then the twilight roster provided coverage. On Early Shift and Late Shift there was generally a Station Senior Sergeant on duty. There was only three of them, so you had them on a rotation basis. On Night Shift I also had supervisory oversight of the Pukekohe Incident patrol or "I Car" as such patrols were commonly referred to. Thankfully that patrol was usually staffed by very experienced members.

Despite being very dedicated and hardworking, these young guys also played pretty hard, sometimes whilst at work. One night the Manurewa "I" Car pulled into the carpark at Papakura for their meal break. While they were eating, the crew of the Papakura "I" Car snuck over to their rival's car and deflated the four tyres. A huge joke but of course next minute a high priority call for service came in for Manurewa. While we were running around trying to find the keys to a spare vehicle the Papakura "I" Car were forced to head off and hold the fort.

Another time I received a note to see one of the Senior Sergeant's an hour after a Night Shift finished. I waited around and then got lined up in the boss's office. It seems that one of the patrol cars had gone in for a routine service the day before and the mechanic got a none too pleasant surprise. When he opened the bonnet of the patrol car the radiator was coated with egg and various citrus fruits. It seemed that my guys had struck again!

On another occasion towards the end of my two-year period in charge I had to pair up a couple of the guys one shift due to a staff shortage. It was widely known that these two didn't get along but, on this occasion, I couldn't do anything about it. Anyway, I decided to pay them a visit when they were parked up at a local service station. I arrived to find them embroiled in a full-on scrap in the patrol car. Sometimes they really did make life difficult for a young NCO, but saying that, I had come to trust each and every one of them with my life.

Sometimes it was like policing the wild west. Occasionally on Night Shift, in which I was usually on my own, I would catch breath around 3.00 am. I would then realise that I had driven about 300 kilometres around the District providing assistance to the other patrols. Sometimes you were numbed to the extent that I would arrive home after a weekend Night Shift, head straight to the fridge and down a beer in one go, followed by another before heading to bed. Glory days!

Early on, I incurred the wrath of the Prosecutor Tony T. I had signed off on a prosecution file for an arrest made by one of my staff. The paperwork appeared alright to me. However, when I arrived back at work the next night the file was back in my in-tray. Stapled to the report form was a sheet of toilet paper (unused I'm pleased to say). In bold letters on the report form were the words "One of these pieces of paper is actually useful!" It was one way to get the point across and clearly something never to be forgotten. Tony T was later to be hugely instrumental in the development of my career as a Prosecutor but we were not off to a great start.

I also inadvertently, did my best to upset the Pukekohe staff. As mentioned earlier they were generally experienced members who could get by without close supervision, and that's the way they liked it. You really needed to watch them when they turned up at Papakura though. The way the wider District seemed to work was that Otahuhu got most of the resources. Some then trickled through to Papakura, and Pukekohe was pretty much on its own. When the Pukekohe "I" Car turned up at the Papakura Police Station it was usually on a raiding mission. Occasionally you had to retrieve furniture and other hardware from their vehicle before they left.

They had a difficult area to police and some "local rules" had developed over time. I went out to visit them early on in my first Night Shift and caught up with them just as they turned over a gang vehicle on the outskirts of Pukekohe. It was a joy to behold. The blue lights went on and the gang car pulled to the side of the road. Several gang members alighted from the vehicle in an orderly fashion before moving to the bonnet or boot of the vehicle. Each assumed the position and were searched for contraband. Clearly this was learnt behaviour, wasn't overly legal, but it was just the way it was. Community Policing at its best, some may say. I did step in over another shortcut though and it did ruffle some feathers. A Noise Control Officer was requesting assistance at a Pukekohe address. As I arrived the Pukekohe "I" car members and the Noise Control Officer were walking up the driveway with the stereo. I enquired about the service of the Abatement Notice. I was told that they didn't use them in Pukekohe; in essence they were actively disregarding the legal process. I ordered them to turn around and return the stereo and to issue the Abatement Notice. I'm pretty sure that they all thought that I had the makings of a fine Commissioned Officer at that point. On another occasion, when we were uplifting a stereo legally, I noticed the biggest guy that I had ever seen asleep on the couch. Everyone was directed to be as quiet as possible for fear of waking this ginormous creature and potentially having a huge battle on our hands.

This was a time before the Intel-based policing that exists today, where computer analysis is almost able to predict when and where crime is going to occur. The local Area Controller was right into directed patrolling. All he had to go on though, was word of mouth and analysis of the written offence reports. Burglaries and unlawful taking of vehicles were always crimes to be targeted. Early Shift had the job of placing coloured pins onto a large map of the District that was on the wall of the Sergeants' office. The theory was that each burglary and unlawful taking would be signified by a coloured pin. That in turn should show hotspots of high crime and therefore areas to target. Unfortunately, that map was also targeted by practical jokers who would move the pins around or add others so that it was a complete and utter waste of time. As they say, statistics are what you choose to make of them.

Another member who was later to be hugely helpful to my career was Uncle Eric, the Court Orderly. Uncle Eric would normally arrive at the station around 5.30am. One of his first jobs was to have a look at the crims who had found their way into the cells. Now Uncle Eric knew the area backwards. He knew the crims; he knew their parents and he knew their children. If you wanted to know anything about the Counties area, you asked Uncle Eric. One night an arrest was causing us quite a bit of grief. The personal details that he had provided just weren't right, but he wasn't budging. Time pressure was mounting because a prosecution file had to be prepared and we also suspected that his correct details was probably going to open a can of worms. We had made no progress when Uncle Eric arrived and first thing, he says upon examining the cell block was "How are you this morning Mr Banks?' Banks replied that he was enjoying having fun with us under his assumed identity. Of course, warrants to arrest and wanted to interviews abounded as well as a sizeable dollop of overtime.

One of the things that kept the public counter busy in those days on Early and Late Shifts was criminals reporting to the station as part of a bail condition. Such things are actively discouraged now because all it really proved, was that we knew what the crim was up to for the few minutes it took to report in. These crims were generally fairly self-centred and didn't like to wait quietly if, heaven forbid, you happened to be dealing with a victim or a law-abiding member of the public. On one occasion a young, fresh-faced guy who looked like butter wouldn't melt in his mouth turned up to report in. As I was searching for his card, I was tempted to give him some grief about his criminal activities. Fortunately, before I did so I saw the word "Murder" alongside 'offence' on his bail reporting card. I couldn't quite believe what I was seeing and thought that someone might be taking the piss. I had to look into this further. I was able to establish that he had been charged with the murder of his mother. It was alleged that he had smashed open her skull with a rock and then he had attempted to set fire to the remains. It did beg the question quite frankly, just what was he doing back in the public arena and darkening the police station doors three times a week, but that's just me, I guess. As they say, you can't always judge a book by its cover.

Here's another example of rolling the dice and calling a matter as you saw it. One Late Shift a report came in that a burglary was in progress a few hundred metres from the station. To be fair it was mentioned that a young guy with a bicycle was involved. A carload of us headed that way from the station. As we entered the street of the crime our headlights were flicked off and we coasted down the middle of the road towards the scene. Sure enough, approaching us was a guy on a bicycle, not wearing a helmet and no headlight showing. That was good enough for us. As he came alongside the patrol car a passenger door was thrust open and took him out. Thank God he was the offender, but again most Officers would have done exactly the same thing.

One Sunday on a Night Shift one of my patrols brought in Dean Wickliffe, one of New Zealand's most notorious criminals. It was for dangerous driving and, as he had no warrants to arrest, he was going to be processed and bailed. I had just finished reading "Mike Bungay on Murder", which featured quite some detail of Wickliffe and also an analysis of the jewellery store robbery in Christchurch which initially put him inside for murder, and then manslaughter on appeal. I introduced myself to Wickliffe and asked him if he wanted a chat and I mentioned Bungay's book. He had no objection, probably because I was certainly no threat to him and, he said that he was pissed off with Bungay because he hadn't been paid for any of the material used in the book. We spent about an hour talking about his upbringing and criminal career. I noted that he was very intense about the jewellery store case and his recall of detail, slanted his way of course, was amazing. A few months after our discussion he was apprehended for another aggravated robbery and he started another long lag. Some leopards never change their spots we are told.

One Saturday evening Night Shift I was called by the Pukekohe "I" car to assist them up at collision crossroads on State Highway One. This was before the expanded motorway system bypassed this area entirely. I arrived to find the patrol talking to an ever-growing number of Black Power members who had turned up in multiple vehicles. Word of mouth had failed our intelligence gatherers as to this situation. The evening before, a Black Power member had allegedly been killed by a Mongrel Mob member in Wairoa. Auckland based members had decided to go down in support and this was the meeting point. They were due to leave about midnight and by that time there would have been about sixty gang members with around twenty vehicles. One of the vehicles was the limousine operated by Wharewaka brothers. In those days when large numbers of gang members travelled anywhere Police usually provided a shadow patrol to limit any fallout to the public. In this case nothing was organised, so I was directed to form an impromptu shadow patrol comprising the Pukekohe "I" car and myself. On this evening I was accompanied by another Constable. We set off around the appointed time although it was painfully slow. Fortunately, there was not a lot of other traffic about. As expected, the gang hierarchy were not unduly concerned by our presence. Their mission was to get to Wairoa to support their brothers and I doubt if they wanted too much drama on the way. We turned down State Highway 2, which was a slight surprise until it became clear that others were to join the convoy at Tauranga, and again at Rotorua. As we pulled into Tauranga the benefit of our presence became apparent. The word was that most of the vehicles needed fuel. We were able to radio ahead and had the Tauranga "I" car meet us at the appointed 24-hour service station. There was a sole attendant on duty. If we had not been there then this guy would probably have had kittens. As it was, about fifteen vehicles filled up with gas and the majority of the gang members stocked up on road trip necessities such as chips, cheezels, luncheon rolls, drinks and chocolate. It was a very lucrative few minutes for the service station and our presence limited any pillaging. Onwards we went, before repeating the exercise at Rotorua. From Rotorua further south through Murupara and then onto the winding roads leading to Lake Waikaremoana. A few kilometres into that journey the radio went dead through lack of coverage and we were on our own. We were also down on staff as well. Word had reached us at Rotorua that the Pukekohe "I" car with one member had to return as the vehicle was required back home in the morning. That left three of us and the Sergeant's vehicle. A couple of gang vehicles gave up on the way and were simply abandoned. One other misjudged a one-way bridge and partially ended up in a creek. It had to be wrenched out by some of the gang members buzzing on chocolate, cola and Christ knows what else. The limousine was making hard work of it. It was simply too long for the narrow metal roads after Murupara. It had to be bounced around several corners often sticking out over the edge. Despite the lack of communication, I was hopeful that we were going to make it through in one piece. If it had been the Mongrel Mob, I would have had more reservations. As it was, I had assessed that I had at my disposal, a Smith & Wesson .38 Special loaded with six rounds and six spare rounds in my pocket. I knew that if they cut up rough, I was going to be forced to take them out three at a time. After what seemed like an eternity, we made it through the night and drew into the metropolis of Wairoa. Local staff were on hand to take over so we bid our farewells to Messrs Wharewaka and Co. and found a motel to get a few hours rest. We then headed back towards Auckland and after dropping off the Pukekohe member arrived back at the Papakura Station about 10.00pm. The Late Shift Senior Sergeant exclaiming that we were just in time to start work. He got a resounding "Bugger off!".

I had been making a few noises about satisfying my interests in the court process. Along the way I had mentioned the prospect of returning to Otahuhu to do that. I must have pushed the right buttons because before too long I was given the call to join Tony T and Uncle Eric.

7   Section One, Papakura 1988.

8 Sergeant's Management & Command Course 1988

5. WHAT'S THIS PROSECUTING LARK ALL ABOUT?

I knew that I had found my calling when I joined the Papakura Prosecutions office. I had always enjoyed going to court as O/C case and had even dabbled with a couple of law papers at one stage. Tony T was an amazing mentor. Unquestionably one of the finest Prosecutors ever produced by the New Zealand Police. He was a little unorthodox at times though. I sat opposite him in our small office and it was not unusual for me to have to duck a file that he had thrown past my ear. Nothing to do with me, it was just how he showed his displeasure with some cases. Uncle Eric did his best to keep Tony T under control. You also knew that every file would contain everything you needed courtesy of Uncle Eric.

Tony T placed complete emphasis upon the weekly List Court. This was the court where new arrests ended up and was also where defended hearings were scheduled from; bearing in mind, status hearing were several years away from existing. The more open and robust nature of status hearings were responsible for resolving a significant number of cases short of a full-blown evidential hearing involving witnesses. Tony, therefore, insisted that he took care of all List Court hearings. It required the funeral of a well-regarded JP, somewhat unhelpfully on a Wednesday

List Day, for me to be trusted with the List after six months in the role. Unusually then, I cut my teeth on defended hearings and depositions hearings. This required me to climb the steep learning curve relating to getting the best from witnesses and mastering legal tactics. This approach is completely contrary to most larger offices where the junior grinds away in Lists for over a year before getting anywhere near running a defended hearing (or Judge Alone Trial as they are now known).

To complete the team, I had the absolute privilege to appear before Judge Ken Richardson, who was the long-standing Resident Judge. He was renowned as being a man's man, although I do suspect that his bark was actually worse than his bite. Many years later he proudly invited me to Chambers to view a gift that the Criminal Bar Association had presented him upon a significant milestone on the bench. It was a beautiful caricature, with an incredible likeness of the Judge, drawn sitting on the bench as a bald eagle (for that was his nickname). Before him was quite a gaggle of turkeys taking up the Counsel benches in a courtroom. It was emblazoned "How can I soar, when I'm surrounded by turkeys". His joy was immeasurable, and I am sure that many years now, after his death, that picture is still displayed with pride in the Richardson household. The beauty of appearing in front of Judge Richardson, was that he was hard on everyone, and that he helpfully dealt to everyone equally. Any professional who appeared in his court lacking preparedness, did so at their peril. The main courtroom at Papakura is designed so that the prosecution bench is hard up against the Registrar's table. For decoration I guess, there is a large wooden lip between the two. I spent quite a bit of time during court hearings ducking under the lip so that the wrath of the Judge would sweep over me and take out any unsuspecting Counsel. Despite my best efforts I still took a few hits. Indeed, after a while, I had suffered just about every rebuke known to the criminal justice system, some of it was even deserved. This grounding though, meant that during my Prosecutions career, none of the literally dozens of Judges that I appeared before, could give me a towelling, quite as bad as Judge Richardson. It gave me the opportunity to be, let's say, quite creative in the future as I acquired the sensation of feeling bulletproof under adversity. It was quite sad though, towards the end of his career when the Judge was battling major health difficulties, particularly with his legs. It got to the stage that when I appeared before him, I would wait for the Registrar to announce "All stand for His Honour the Judge". If it took the Judge longer than about thirty seconds to get up the step and along to his seat on the bench then it was going to be one of those days, and I slid even further under the lip on the table. The Judge was a master at telling off defendants and I'm sure that he managed to scare quite a few of them back to the straight and narrow. The Judge did have a sense of humour though. One day he was tearing an absolute strip off a defendant whose surname was "Honey". After what seemed like an eternity of dressing down the Judge screamed out "Now look here Honey!". He realised what he had said about the same time as the public gallery got up enough courage to snigger a little. Everyone including the Judge then had a jolly good laugh. I even dragged my head out of hiding to share the moment.

When Tony T was on leave, I had the audacity to challenge a decision of Judge Richardson. For a while it looked pretty good as Crown Law even filed the appeal papers before having second thoughts and withdrawing them. This in effect, hung me out to dry as the Judge was aware that I wasn't towing the party line. All Tony T would say when he came back was "You did what!!!". The comeback on me was that for a period of about 6 months, I couldn't take a trick in front of the Judge.

I recall that the following incident occurred during that period when I was sent to Coventry. When you prepared a defended hearing list you made small notes on the cover of each file that are legible only to you. The reason being, that when you headed over to court, bright and early and set up for the pending disasters ahead, the lawyers start to swarm. From a distance, because fingers are not allowed, they seek out any trace of weakness. It was not uncommon to turn up to court and a file had not yet arrived from an Officer in Charge. One of my great colleagues Colin, perfected a system around this by padding out files with multitudes of blank paper to give the outward impression that everything was okay. After you had set up the files in court you then awaited the arrival of the Officers involved in the cases who gave a final update as to whether the witnesses had turned up or not. When Judge Richardson stormed in on this particular day, the cases were called through, and it became apparent that due to one reason or another, only a drink drive case was ready to proceed immediately. Normally the Judge would retire for a few minutes after the call through of cases to let everyone catch their breath, but on this occasion the Judge ploughed right on without a break. I was told to call the Officer in my drink drive case. There was no response from the back of the court. A couple of other Officers scurried about and all I was able to be advised was that the Officer had been at court but couldn't be located now. That was all the opportunity I was given and the charge was dismissed; the drink driver walking out with a smirk on his face. The Officer had actually been present prior to the call through, but this being his first case and all, he faced the need for an urgent call of nature. Now, as anyone would know, the male toilets in the foyer of the Papakura District Court were disgusting. He had chosen the safer option of heading across to the Police Station next door where he seriously reduced the chance of catching something (other than a criminal). Where the Officer fell down though, was in not telling anyone where he was going and for potentially how long. I was sure that even Judge Richardson would have conceded that a visit to the loo for a nervous one was a good reason for a short adjournment. Sometimes you just have to accept that the law is a bit of an arse.

I was called into Chambers one day after List Court. I wondered if it was a social visit or was I about to get bounced around a bit. I was invited in and the Judge pronounced "Your diversion scheme is racist.". All I could say was "Pardon?" He said that he had been at a conference and one of the speakers had declared that the

Police Diversion Scheme was racist. I advised the Judge that I would go back to the office and get our records. I returned a few minutes later. I explained to the Judge that race meant so little to us that we didn't even record it on our diversion return. However, I invited the Judge to accept that some surnames indicate whether the person was probably Maori, Polynesian, Asian and indeed European. Not wildly scientific but it was all I could do. He accepted that and scanned through the list of names before handing the records back to me. "I knew they were making it up", was his observation.

One late afternoon on a stinking hot summer's day I headed over to court to see how Tony T was getting on. It was a scene I will remember forever. Present were a defendant represented by a specialist drink drive lawyer, Tony T, the Registrar and Judge Richardson. It was too hot for anyone to be bothered to watch from the public gallery. Let's just say that English was not the first language of the lawyer and his deep gravelly tone made understanding almost impossible. The Judge stared ahead with a wizened glare, clearly wishing that he was at home tending to his farm. Tony T was reclined back in his chair, arms stretched down to the side whilst staring at the ceiling. He just wished that he was anywhere else that involved a beer. Oblivious to this, the lawyer was just waxing on, trying to make his point. Sometimes you were pleased that others were doing the hard yards instead of you.

Another hot afternoon in List Court illustrated some of the pedantic rules that existed in the criminal justice system.

Nowadays, most Judges will allow pleas to be entered, particularly if the defendant is represented by Counsel, without having the charges readout. Back in these times though every charge was read out. A defendant appeared charged with over 120 counts of fraud. We all settled in for the long haul as the Registrar began to read out the charges. Now, fraud charges are fairly long and repetitive. After about forty-five minutes of a charge being read and a guilty plea entered, most of us present were considering self harm. Incredibly and for no apparent reason, the defendant then slipped in a not guilty plea. I have no idea why; I don't think he even knew. It could just have been an attempt to break up the monotony. None of us except the Registrar knew where we were up to and there were frantic attempts to work out which charge had actually been denied. to. After everyone got back up to speed, we all settled down for another forty-five minutes of trauma just hoping that the defendant didn't pull the same trick again.

Occasionally, occurrences do highlight that it pays to be careful to avoid mistakes. A defendant was called from custody. He appeared and Counsel rose to indicate that they had instructions to appear for the defendant. The charge was put to the defendant and he pleaded guilty. I read the summary of facts to the court. Nowadays, it is rare for a summary to be read due to time constraints. I showed the defendant his criminal history which was confirmed and the Judge then went on to sentence him. A few minutes later the defendant was recalled because he was not in fact the person who had committed the offence that he had been sentenced on. He had simply been put in the dock and he agreed without question to everything that was going on. I'm confident that this was not a ruse by a clever defendant hoping to get released under the identity of another; no, this guy was just thick. It did beg the question as to how the lawyer got it so wrong, as he was the only one to have actually seen the defendant before his appearance.

On one occasion I headed back to the office after a lengthy List day. Fortunately, I decided to do some paperwork on some of my files before heading home. A few minutes later my phone rang and I was asked to return to the court. Apparently, a cleaner had started work in the cell block area after everyone had left and had found a defendant languishing in one of the cells awaiting his time in court. Luckily the Judge had the same idea as me regarding the paperwork, and we were able to reconvene the court and the defendant was none the wiser. You can be rest assured that there was a bit of a tongue lashing for the Escort Staff.

As we were getting our files prepared, usually on a busy List day, we would often be contacted by the media who were searching for anything newsworthy. They were supposed to come out on occasions but Papakura was such a long way and they preferred to let their fingers do the walking. It just so happened that on this day there was a defendant with the surname 'Constable' appearing on an indecent assault charge. You guessed it, the Herald was advised, when they rudely interrupted us, that a Constable was appearing on indecent assault. Well, this was music to the ears of the media. Upon arrival at the court, it was standing room only. We handed over the press copy of the charge to the media who were somewhat forlorn when they realised what they had fallen for. We didn't seem to get many calls from them after that.

Every few years Uncle Eric would have the urge to do a bit of a tidy up. On one such occasion he came up from behind his desk clutching a court list from about eight years prior. What he discovered highlighted the insular nature of Papakura as a community. The old court list that Uncle Eric had discovered, bore a striking similarity to the current one. The same old families appearing time and time again. So much for attempts to curb recidivism.

About half way through my tenure at Papakura, Judge Augusta Wallace arrived as an additional Resident Judge. I noted that she was in remarkably good fettle despite the savage attack on her by a youth in court at Otahuhu that almost took her life a year or so earlier. I really liked her style and she was a great complement to Judge Richardson. On occasions after the court had adjourned for morning tea, the side door would slowly open and I would be beckoned into the Judge's common room. Judge Richardson would be seated there, Judge Wallace would have a huge pot of tea in her hand, and I was asked if I took one lump or two. It was lovely stuff to be able to interact with such legends in this way.

Judge Wallace presided over one of my cases that unofficially must go down as one of the lengthiest District Court cases ever. The case itself was relatively simple, but the identities involved created a perfect storm. The defendant was charged with intentional damage and assault with a weapon relating to a neighbourly dispute on a rural property. It started when one party (the complainant), needed access so that they could transport in a minor dwelling down a shared driveway. A couple of branches were cut from a tree without consulting the neighbour. The neighbour's reaction was to chainsaw down a stand of fifteen tall poplar trees. A physical confrontation ensued in which the complainant maintained that he was struck on the shoulder by the defendant who was wielding an iron bar. There was a connection between the defendant and his Legal Counsel to the extent that this case was never going to settle. It was set down for a two-day defended hearing. At the commencement of the hearing, it was apparent that this wasn't going to be sorted out promptly. Despite her best efforts Judge Wallace was not able to control Counsel and we spent considerable periods of time in her Chambers with the Judge tearing strips off him. We headed back into court and clearly the blows of the Judge had not landed because Counsel would be at it again and back to Chambers, we would go. The allocated two days passed with very little progress. Further dates were scheduled, so that we ultimately ended up with fifteen sittings days over a nine-month period. In hindsight, the defendant played a ruse that was several years before, the one run by O J Simpson in his famous trial. You will be familiar with the claim "If the glove doesn't fit, then you must acquit". In our trial the defendant was maintaining that the iron bar was simply too heavy for him to have used it as alleged, due to a shoulder injury. Despite my objections the Judge allowed the defendant to demonstrate this from the witness box. His feeble attempts to raise the bar brought a tear to my eye and I thought to myself that it probably wasn't the only thing he couldn't raise! The Judge did allow me to rebut this however. I was able to call the very diminutive Court Registrar who was able to wave the bar around like a 'Ninja Warrior'. After all of the drama the decision was a little strange. The defendant had to be convicted on the intentional damage charge as there was no real justification for chopping down the stand of poplar trees. Despite the defendant being at pains, literally, to show that he could not have used the bar as a weapon, the Judge found that he could, probably as a result of my rebuttal witness. However, she found, without any claim from the defendant, that he acted in self-defence and that charge was dismissed. Counsel made a muted claim about costs, but the Judge shut him down with a stare that screamed "Just you try me!"

A couple of days out from a List Court I had a call from a QC, who wanted to meet regarding a client who was to appear in that list. The QC arrived and from the outset continually referred to the defendant as His Royal Highness. I was fairly sure that none of the Windsor's had been in town and up to no good. If they had, it was of course another opportunity for a royal encounter. I sought an explanation. Apparently, there is a small island that is part of the Fijian group, that parted ways as a result of the coup. This group of people had their own, albeit small sovereign monarchy. Our defendant was the king who had found himself living in exile in New Zealand. Our interest had arisen as a result of his actions during a vehicle stop conducted by one of our patrols. It became apparent that the QC wanted the charges withdrawn, although it appeared more so on diplomatic, rather than legal grounds. After a few more references to His Royal Highness, the QC left. I knew that Judge Wallace was going to be on the bench and I wondered what she was going to make of all this. The day arrived and the defendant was called. Wow, he strode to the dock wearing the most amazing, white John Travolta suit. All it needed was disco lights and soundtrack and the scene would have been complete. The QC jumped to his feet and introduced himself, although he was well known to the Judge and others in the courtroom. I was just waiting for the fun to begin and then it started. Every submission commenced with reference to His Royal Highness. The Judge seemed to be having some difficulty putting this all together until she stopped Counsel and wanted an explanation about this royal connection. So, we heard it all again, after which the Judge pointed out that if there wasn't a connection to the Windsor's then he wasn't going to be afforded any titles in her court. This just went in one ear and out of the other for the QC who continued with the royal reference. To be fair to Counsel, he was being paid to play up the royal aspect for his client, but it was getting no traction with the Judge. There was even a short adjournment taken by the Judge so that the QC could get his act together. No improvement after the break as the rule of money clearly outweighs the rule of law. The case was ultimately set down for a hearing a few months later. A compromise of sorts was reached when the driver took the rap, and His Royal Highness walked free.

The practices of the court change often depending upon who is in charge. This raised concern at the time, but it was someone's bright idea that any mentally impaired persons should be dealt with by the Judge in Chambers. I'm not talking about the courtroom minus members of the public, I'm talking about the Judge's actual Chambers. Now as a rule of thumb, most people are well behaved and respectful at court. Some do have an axe to grind on an issue dear to them, or don't accept jurisdiction of the court on sovereign grounds, but by and large behave themselves. The introduction of searching of all persons attending court is testament to the fact that it can be a dangerous place. What I have found is that most people have enough clues that if you behave at court, then you have more chance with the Judge, than if you were acting up. Even hardened gang members seem to follow the rules around the expected standard of behaviour. There are exceptions to every rule and in this instance, it is young people and mentally impaired persons. My observation is that some young people are so self-centred and lacking of any appreciation of consequences for their actions to the extent that anything is possible. The prime example is the terrible attack upon Judge Wallace. Unpredictability is what to expect with young people at court. The other group likely to cause problems are mentally impaired persons. It goes with the territory that if someone is harbouring under a mental illness then it is likely that they are not aware of their actions through no real fault of their own. So, as a result of the bizarre determination made by someone in Court Management myself, a Police Escort, Counsel, and a mentally impaired person squeezed into Judge Wallace's Chambers for the court hearing. There was hardly room to swing a cat but we got on with it anyway. No great problem arose until the defendant twigged to the fact that he was not going to be heading home any time soon, and he took a swing at the Escort Officer. Next minute the Escort Officer, myself, and I even vaguely recall Counsel, were scrapping it out with the defendant. The Judge had been tipped off her seat onto the floor and statutes were literally flying off the bookshelf onto her. After what seemed to be an eternity, order was restored but the Judge's Chambers resembled a war zone. Suffice to say we didn't do that anymore.

The Escort Staff had to deal with some pretty awful occurrences even if the odd prisoner was left behind after the day. One List Court had to be interrupted when a well-known defendant, who was borderline mentally impaired, for no apparent reason, started to rip his throat apart whilst waiting in the cells. Before long he had given himself a full-scale tracheostomy, without sedation and there was blood everywhere. I did see this guy a few years later at the Manukau DC when he was sentenced to twelve years on a home invasion. It would be interesting to know what's up with him now.

On a lighter note, Uncle Eric had a bit of fun with the prisoners one day shortly after a general election and John Banks had been appointed as Police Minister. Now Uncle Eric was incredibly well known to the punters as mentioned earlier, as most are repeat business. Uncle Eric had just received an order of carrots that came in a huge box purchased from a court staff member who was taking advantage of the fertile soil out Pukekohe way. By midday the prisoners were starting to rark up and began demanding that Uncle Eric get on with sorting out their lunch. Uncle Eric announced to the hungry prisoners that directions had arrived from John Banks that healthy lunches were the way forward, and that they weren't going to be getting pies anymore. Well, there was just about a riot when Uncle Eric showed the prisoners the box of carrots that John Banks had kindly sent him. The prisoners not too politely, indicated to Uncle Eric what he could do with his carrots. There was a bit of a standoff for about ten minutes before the meanest ugliest prisoner called out "Uncle, give us those carrots please, we're hungry." It does seem that learnt behaviour can be changed with simple incentives.

I was running defended hearings one day when it became apparent that the court was adjourning at strange times. The usual sitting times for court are from 10.00 am to 11.30am. From 11.45 am to 1.00pm. The afternoon session is from 2.15pm to 3.30pm. Hopefully things had wrapped up by this stage otherwise 3.45pm to finish. On this day the adjournments were at completely different times and about 35 minutes apart for around 5 minutes duration. I initially had some sympathy for the Judge who I suspected might be suffering from a bad curry although sometimes he did return to court looking rather pleased with himself. It later transpired that the Judge had a number of horses running at a race meeting down the line that day, and it probably appeared more professional if he adjourned to listen to each race rather than wear a radio earpiece. Good on him for this classic example of multi-tasking.

Whilst I was at Papakura Prosecutions, I qualified for the 14-year long service and good conduct medal. A regionwide ceremony was held at the Fickling Centre in Three Kings. It was very fitting to me that my medal was presented, by none other than Her Honour Judge Wallace. By then, she had been the recipient of a Royal Honour and was officially known as Dame Augusta Wallace. However, we all affectionately referred to her as Gussie. In future years, my 21-year clasp was presented to me by Commissioner MacDonald at Harlech House and my 28-year clasp by Auckland Mayor Len Brown at the Manukau Police Station. I will refrain from mentioning the 35-year award at this stage and save it for a later chapter. Some Officers speak of receiving their long service awards in the post from their supervisor. I'm pleased that my experiences were a little more memorable.

My time at Papakura came to an end in 1995, and rotation was still in vogue at the time. A vacancy had arisen for a Section Supervisor at Howick, so I jumped at that, rather than being placed into a role than didn't suit my circumstances. Interestingly one of my close colleagues in the office at that time kept his head down and was still there when he retired twenty years later.

6. I THINK I STILL WANT TO BE A PROSECUTOR...IN FACT I KNOW THAT I DO.

My stories over the next four years are somewhat sparse. I was unsettled, and unsure just how long I could stick at the job. This probably explains why I went through three roles over this period. In reality, I just wanted to be a Prosecutor, something that I knew I was good at. My perception was, that the Department didn't see Prosecutions as being a long-term career option. This of course, changed in 1999 with the advent of the Police Prosecutions Service, but still not early enough for me. I even applied for a position as a Surveillance Officer at the newly built Harrahs Casino, later to be known as Sky City. They were being very cagey about salaries on offer. After one testing session about one hundred of us were in a large room. Some suits at the front asked if anyone had any questions. Someone wanted to know about parking; someone else about meals. I then asked what they were paying. You could have heard a pin drop in the room. Management were still because they were hoping to avoid such a god-awful question, and the other applicants were grateful because finally someone had the guts to ask it. The end result, after a lot of hand wringing and creative accounting, was that even the team leader would be on about two thirds of what the Police were presently paying me. I explained that didn't do it for me, and clearly, I wasn't what they were looking for. I'm not entirely sure just who they were hoping to employ, at that rate.

Howick

One good thing about returning to the role of Section Supervisor after some experience as a Prosecutor, is that you can confidently make decisions regarding the quality of arrests. I was able to turn up at incidents and be advised of an arrest. A quiet word would be had with the arresting Officer, to establish the available evidence. It was not unusual for us to then kick suspects loose. Over the years, I have encountered too many, predominantly young Officers, who would arrive at my desk with all of the woes of the world on their shoulders. It is not uncommon in the Police for senior staff to swoop in, and lock up offenders, and then pass them off to junior staff, supposedly to give them experience. These were the days when Prosecutions was not set up as robustly for early case management review, and files may not be properly assessed for evidential sufficiency, until the day before a defended hearing. These young Officers were then left for months, not knowing how they were supposed to prove the case against the defendant. When I heard of such cases, I would make an analysis of the available evidence, confirm that nothing further could be obtained and then often make a decision to 'kill' the case. The earlier that is done, the less prospect of adverse comment, and potentially, costs. It is about evidence, when all said and done, not simply a numbers game. Some dead horses are not worth flogging.

Howick was a good station to work from, being close to home and all. For eight years, I had been travelling around thirty kilometres each way to Papakura, only some of it on a shift transport allowance. Having a commute of less than five minutes was a real bonus. The Howick catchment was always considered to be the quietest of the areas within the Counties Manukau District. Probably true, but all the staffing level enabled me to put out, was an Incident Patrol, a Traffic Patrol (the merger with the MOT having occurred in 1992) and a one person "Q" car, during daylight hours. The area stretched from the Tamaki River to the west and Beachlands Maraetai to the east. There was a sole charge Constable based at Beachlands, but the Howick staff went out for anything serious, or for an ice cream on a warm Sunday afternoon at Maraetai Beach. The local shitheads knew about staffing levels. One Saturday Night Shift an urgent call came in for a job at Maraetai. The "I" car and myself responded. It ended up being a hoax and when we returned an hour later to the main street of Howick, all of the rubbish bins on both sides of the road were on fire. It was pretty impressive and resembled a scene from one of the Mad Max movies.

As a front-line Police Officer death, is never far away from you; from fatal vehicle crashes to other accidents, intentional deaths and those from natural causes. The smell of the Middlemore Hospital mortuary is something that I will never forget. I recall back on Section at Otahuhu, one young cop went to a sudden death of an old bloke, who let's say hadn't been seen for quite a while. We never saw the cop again after that. In one seven-day period at Howick my staff attended five self-inflicted deaths, three of them involving young people and one a serving Police member. Sadly, there were also a couple of cot deaths. I made arrangements for counselling to be made available to any Officer who wished to avail themselves. True to form, there were no takers from those hard-arsed bastards.

You are encouraged not to rock the boat too much but sometimes it has to be done. You will recall from my Enquiry days at Otara, that I was happy to not be constrained by the rigours of the Children and Young Persons and Their Families Act 1989. Well, that statute was now law. One day, I was the acting Senior Sergeant at the Howick Police Station. I was made aware that a youth from Otara had been arrested for burglary and he was about to be interviewed. I asked whether the young person's parents had been advised and did they wish to participate. I was told that things weren't done that way at Howick. Apparently, the local JP was on his way to sit in as a Nominated Person. I told the staff that it wasn't going to happen like that on my watch, and as the kid didn't know the phone number, they were going to have to head over to Otara with him to find the parents. Lower lips droopy all round, but the law is the law. The JP arrived and hit the roof. I apologised for wasting his time but he just wasn't having it and was wandering around advising all and sundry of my pedigree. I finally got him to leave and started to field concerns from staff because I might have compromised his soft touch for warrant applications. Fortunately, the actual Senior Sergeant agreed with my actions and after a few weeks' things blew over. Interestingly I encountered the same JP when he was sitting at both the Otahuhu and then Manukau District Courts. We got on really well. I never raised the matter with him, but I suspect that he had forgotten about it or possibly he actually realised that he was in the wrong.

One occurrence gave me a hold over a now very senior member of the Justice Community. As if things weren't busy enough, I was required to assign summons files periodically to the staff to complete over the following few days. On the following Sunday, I was just settling in to lunch when a junior member advised me that he had served a summons on a cop that morning. First off, I established that it was for careless use of a motor vehicle, probably as a result of a Departmental crash. These were usually served by one of the investigators, not dished out amongst the rank and file, so that was unusual. Secondly, I pointed out to the Officer that the Summary Proceedings Act 1957 prevented the service of such summonses on a Sunday, probably to do with the day of rest and all that. However, the statute went on to say that incorrect service did not invalidate the process. The server was liable to a $40 fine. I told the Officer that there was no need for that and simply gave him a warning. It was partly my fault anyway, because I wrongly assumed that staff knew that summonses shouldn't be served on a Sunday.

A few weeks later all hell broke loose. The Traffic Inspector demanded my presence at District Headquarters. Upon arrival, he began ranting about some conspiracy to have the prosecution of an Officer fail. When the Inspector was able to reduce his blood pressure and give his popping veins a rest, I was able to establish what had happened. The Traffic Prosecutor had attended the JP Traffic Court with files that included one for the cop who had been charged. The case was called and the cop was represented by a very experienced lawyer who I knew quite well. It's likely that his fee was being taken care of by the Police Association. I have no issues with that as it is part of being a member. The lawyer advised the JP's that the summons had been served on a Sunday, and that they should dismiss the charge. I wasn't there, so I can only speculate that the lawyer only read out part of the applicable section of the Summary Proceeding Act 1957.[1] The Prosecutor apparently fumbled about without looking at the statute and failed to raise any objection. The JP's accepted what the experienced lawyer was saying and didn't see the need to check the statute either. The charge was dismissed and the cop walked free. The Prosecutor returned to the office and the conspiracy theory began. The Inspector clearly wanted my guts for garters, so I put the brakes on and advised that I would respond with a written report. Rightly or wrongly, I didn't feel the need for any legal advice. I prepared the report carefully detailing the situation as outlined, and also attached a copy of the applicable section. Not surprisingly I didn't find myself being charged with attempting to defeat the course of justice. In fact, I heard nothing at about this ever again. It would have been nice if the Inspector had notified me that he was incorrect.

---

[1] Section 203(3) Summary Proceedings Act 1957

I have raised this occurrence on a couple of occasions with the lawyer, who has now moved on to bigger and better things. He mentioned something about doing what had to be done. I personally don't believe misleading the court to be one of those things. This may highlight the difference between a lawyer and a Police Officer. **It might pay to remember this paragraph when you read the final chapter.** On that point, here is a spoiler alert. The ride might get a little bumpy as the end of this book approaches.

Otara

My return to Otara was to a strange sort of gig. I had been appointed to the role of Station Sergeant which involved the line supervision of the three Community Constables and three Youth Aid Officers. They were all experienced and well regarded in the community, but supervision of staff in these roles is a little like herding cats. I really enjoyed working with the Station Senior Sergeant. He was clearly a 'blue flamer', but was a really caring leader. I'm not at all surprised that he is now part of the Police Executive. I was also tasked with liaising with the multitude of community and youth organisations within the area. Otara had endured a fairly bad rap over the years. The community organisations that I encountered, such as Maori Wardens and Cross Power Ministries to unfairly name just a couple, really had their hearts in the right place and were beginning to make quite a difference. My observation was that Otara as a community had turned a corner with the problems of a few years back gaining some maturity. It was fair to say that Clendon had surpassed Otara as the problem child of the District.

The Senior Sergeant wanted something done about a troublesome night-club based over at the Otara Town Centre. Together we collated a myriad of attendances by the team Policing Unit and others and an application was filed seeking to cancel the liquor licence. I ran the hearing which lasted a couple of days. Strangely, the Judge was more interested in the fact that the licensee could only speak Vietnamese rather than the voluminous instances of disorder we could prove. The Judge determined that a licensee must have a good grasp of the intricacies of the Sale of Liquor Act 1989 and in the absence of proof that he did, the Judge cancelled the licence. A great result even if it was on grounds from left field. Before long I had been poached by the brother of my boss at Otara and I was heading into the District Headquarters as Community Relations Coordinator.

District Headquarters

The role of District Community Relations Coordinator was potentially bigger than Africa and was very difficult to quantify results. Saying that, my new boss, who like his brother, was a decent caring man, pretty much let me get on with things as I saw fit. I was required to maintain contact with Neighbourhood Support at a District level as well as other groups such as Alcohol Healthwatch. I wasn't sure if it was part of the brief, but I also created opportunities to provide crime prevention advice to businesses and community groups as that role had earlier been disestablished. One of the either positive or negative aspects of the role, depending upon your viewpoint, was that if any senior manager didn't wish to attend any Local Body or Governmental meeting, then I would go in their place. I also had quite a list of meetings that were mine to attend as of right. This was a time when Government agencies and the Council were not as concerned about wasteful spending. I was therefore on a constant round of provided morning teas, luncheons and afternoon teas. This was starting to take a toll on my waistline. I was also beginning to gain some appreciation for the term "fat cats".

It was also a period where the Police neglected to provide vehicles for its Community Constables, expecting the community to provide sponsored vehicles instead. I was able to call in a couple of favours and during my time was able to source vehicles from Manukau Nissan, South Auckland Ford and Telecom Directories.

I was assigned to the failed "Sweetwaters Festival" of 1999. It was an absolute disaster, so much so that the promoter later served a prison sentence for fraud. My role was to keep a tab upon the security arrangements. It became readily apparent that very few of the hired guns were actually licenced, so it came down to gathering the evidence. The festival itself was plagued with problems right from the start. Blistering heat turned to torrential downpours, turning everything to mud. One of the chefs for the kitchen providing food for Police staff was arrested for indecent assault on the first night. That meant Police had to find a new caterer at short notice which I'm told came at quite a price. The next night, the head electrician spun out, and was located dancing on a roof but not in a good way. He was wheeled off under the Mental Health Act. When it was all done and dusted, I had the evidence, so I went after the licence of the security company involved in the fiasco. It was a bit of a hollow victory in the end because they went bankrupt around the same time, but I got their licence nonetheless.

After a while I got to the stage that I just couldn't attend another community meeting and paint a picture of rosiness, knowing deep down, that for any number of reasons, we just couldn't deliver what the community expected. A quick word with my understanding boss and I was heading back to Prosecutions, this time at Otahuhu.

7. THE RETURN OF THE PRODIGAL SON.

I wasn't a complete stranger to the Prosecutions Office at Otahuhu. Some there knew me as a country cousin from my time at Papakura; some even earlier than that. I don't know if my previous boss knew, but for a year or so, I had a cosy arrangement with Prosecutions that I would relieve if they were short, and I had nothing else on. This allowed me to keep my hand in, whilst Prosecutions was able to call upon an experienced operative, whenever needed. This was an amazing office to join. Any team that can boast the calibre of Laurie Ohms, Colin Graham and Eardley Dijkstra on the roster, equates to the All Blacks on steroids. Add Richard Spendelow to that line up when we got to Manukau, and it was a real dream team. Otahuhu was a great place to work, with an emphasis upon practical jokes. You had to be careful that your suitcase hadn't been supplemented with phonebooks or a dumbbell before heading to court. One classic prank, involved a member intercepting a pair of new pants that one of the ladies had put in the drycleaners for the legs to be hemmed. She had pinned them to the desired length, before the joker took another ten centimetres off that. Somewhat surprisingly, the drycleaners did what was asked. To her credit, the female Prosecutor took it fairly well, and even wore the three-quarter pants over to court. Later at Manukau, they had a fine way to promote discussion in the office, which included a seating plan comprising "The Creche" for newbies, "Wisteria Lane" for the middle band, and "Paratai Drive" for the elite.

I had arrived back at Prosecutions in time to see the introduction of the Police Prosecutions Service. The new structure provided a level of independence and diversity, that had not previously been seen. The command structure of each PPS office reported to Police National Headquarters directly, via an Area Manager rather than being part of the local District. This enabled disagreements to be addressed at the appropriate level, rather than simply a high-ranking District Officer calling the shots. The new structure also enabled the recruitment of external Barristers as Prosecutors. The upshot of this was the potential for differing points of view to be considered, as it is well known that Police Officers tend to sing from the same song sheet. It took some time, but a career progression framework was introduced so that Prosecutions was able to be viewed as a long-term career path. So much for me bailing from Papakura after five years, due to the spectre of rotation hanging over me.

Before I really got cracking with this stint at Otahuhu, some of us were rostered for duty at the APEC conference in September 1999. I was assigned an Otahuhu section and we were on Late Shift for the week, in the environs of the conference venue at Aotea Square. I couldn't believe the first afternoon when we arrived and we were each handed a brown paper bag. Inside were a couple of wilted sandwiches, a cookie and an apple. I asked the Logistics Officer what it was and was told that it was our meal. How things had changed. During the Springbok Tour we were treated to two cooked meals a night, from the Army kitchen whilst on duty at Eden Park. Concert duties had always involved a cooked meal. It was obvious that the budget only extended to the rich and famous, and not those doing the hard yards. I don't know how the Police Association ever let them get away with it.

Our standard duty involved patrolling around the fenced perimeter to Aotea Square, although in reality there wasn't a lot happening. One of my staff got something to tell the grandkids about, when our Section was chosen at short notice to clear the way for Prime Minister Jenny Shipley. The staff member had the task of opening the door of the ministerial limo, and to give a salute without looking like a complete idiot.

It was really interesting to watch the assorted media crews do their live to air broadcasts, a few metres over our shoulders. One Australian network was hilarious. It comprised a presenter, a cameraman and a sound guy. Each had a cold beer in hand, and it was apparent that it wasn't their first. Suddenly the director walked over and did the finger countdown. Beer bottles went onto the ground, out of shot and the broadcast began. When the job was completed a couple of minutes later, the entire crew were back into their beers. The TV3 crew were a little more circumspect, although after their live to air cross, Carol headed straight off, whilst John hit it off with the crew like it was old home week.

At short notice, one afternoon during the conference, we were sent down to the Richmond Boat Club on Westhaven

Drive. This is a beautiful location with the Harbour Bridge looming large in the landscape. Apparently, Madeleine Albright, the US Secretary of State, had a meeting scheduled at the venue. The problem was, that there were so many coaches blocking the narrow access to the marina that Ms Albright's motorcade couldn't get in. Not an issue, this was New Zealand after all. It was a beautiful day so she decided to walk the 200 metres or so to the Boat Club. My Section was scattered around just outside of the venue. As she approached on foot, it was apparent to anyone that she was an extremely powerful woman. However, she was also accompanied by a security detail of about eight staff, armed to the teeth. The looks that they gave us were fearsome, and it was apparent that they don't really enjoy impromptu changes to their routine. I swear that if any of us had sneezed at the wrong time, we would have been filled with lead. Fortunately, everyone behaved themselves, and we lived to fight another day.

On the final evening we arrived at Aotea Square to a completely changed environment. A farewell dinner was to be held in the Auckland Town Hall, which was in the corner of our perimeter. The first thing we noticed upon arrival, were snipers on the roof of office buildings overlooking the Town Hall. Not something that you see every day in Auckland. There was a black SUV with tinted windows parked near our position. We got talking to one of the occupants, who resembled a real-life Action Man. The best piece of advice he gave us was; that if any shooting started, we should just hit the deck, and hope for the best. Each of us had a nibble on a sandwich well past it's used by date, and contemplated what we had been told. President Clinton arrived, but all we got was a fairly distant view. Word has it, that earlier in the week he had demanded that his motorcade screech to a halt along Parnell Road, so that he could go do some shopping for Hillary, or was that Monica?

There was another drama at the end of proceedings. The Sultan of Brunei advised his detail, that he had eaten far too much, and that he would be walking to his hotel, now the Grand Millennium, on Mayoral Drive. The motorcade was despatched elsewhere, and arrangements were made for safe passage through the Mayoral Drive underpass. The Sultan twigged onto this and explained that he would be crossing the road like a normal person. The security detail was having kittens by this stage, but dutifully complied. Fortunately, Mayoral Drive on a Sunday evening is not terribly busy, and the package was able to be delivered to bed, safe and sound.

After the fun and games of APEC I was able to return to being a Prosecutor. The Otahuhu District Court was decommissioned in 2000. All of us were then relocated to the newly opened Manukau District Court, to continue our careers. Everyone involved with these courts have their own stories, which are regaled often. I've put together some of mine, which are by no means exhaustive. I trust that you enjoy them and obtain some level of insight into the life of a Prosecutor.

8. ARE YOU LOOKING FOR SOMETHING?

The court system is by no means perfect. It can be painfully slow, burdened by paperwork, and bogged down by niceties. Therefore, it is incumbent, for the participants to do their very best to achieve at least a semblance of justice for the victims, witnesses and defendants. It is expected that Judges will be authoritative, but also reasonable and fair. They should dispense justice equally to all, and show some humility whilst going about it. It's fair to say that some achieve these expectations better than others. Lawyers generally get a pretty bad rap. The whole profession is widely regarded as dishonest and criminal lawyers are viewed as being at the bottom of the heap. Where people go wrong in their assessment though, is that they forget to acknowledge that a lawyer, has a legal and ethical duty to act in the best interests of their client…. **according to the rule of law.** However, it is by not adhering to the emphasised portion that some lawyers come unstuck. And it's not just right-thinking members of society who are scathing of lawyers. Lawyers also get it in the neck from some of their clients, whose expectations far exceed what is actually possible. The Court Staff are the glimmer of hope in the court process. Acknowledged as generally not being remunerated to the level that they actually play; the whole system would grind to a halt without them. It is a well-regarded rule that you do not give Court Staff a hard time, hence the point of this little story. Prosecutors are often regarded as inferior by both Judges and lawyers. Demands made by the bench upon Prosecutors, would simply not be tolerated by Defence Counsel, supported by appellate courts. Saying that, most Prosecutors are resilient in the splendour that they do their duty for the good guys, rather than languishing on the dark side. The top dogs of the lawyers are Queen's Counsel or QC's for short. It is not unusual for some of them to be referred to, using the same abbreviation 'QC', but the words have a completely different connotation!

One such practitioner, and a prized one at that, turned up at the Otahuhu District Court one day. Looking resplendent in his beautifully tailored three-piece suit, he certainly stood out. Let's just say that some of the resident lawyers were strangers to their local drycleaner. This guy strode purposefully to the Registrar's desk, just oozing arrogance. His first mistake was about to happen; he demanded that his client's case be called first. Technically speaking, he was correct as his status allowed him to jump the queue. However, there are ways and means of achieving this. His approach failed the attitude test by quite some distance. Now, I must point it out here, that I was not a protagonist in this event, nor was I a conspirator. However, I was about the courtroom that day, so can confirm what actually occurred. Immediately after the approach from the QC, the eyes of the Registrar met those of the Prosecutor. Nothing was, or needed to be said. With a little sleight of hand, the court file disappeared, as though David Copperfield had just breezed on through.

Shortly afterwards, the Judge entered the courtroom and greeted the QC like it was old home week. The Registrar was asked by the Judge to call the learned QC's matter. The Judge was advised that the file hadn't yet been received from the court office. Instructions were issued to hurry things up, so that the QC could be on his way. A few minutes later word was received from the office to the extent that it was their belief, that the file should already be in court. A search of the files came up short, and the Judge was advised that it was 'missing'. This was a frequently used term at the Otahuhu District Court in those days, and has continued to be so used in most courts ever since. 'Missing' simply indicated that the file would probably turn up at some stage. Apologies were extended from the bench to the QC, who was beginning to look somewhat less dapper in his nice little three piece.

Time marched on, and no progress was being made. Anyone who has had anything at all to do with the legal system, will know that it operates on paper and screeds of it, at that. Without a file, and therefore something for the Judge to write on, you just weren't going to get the job done. Defendant after defendant appeared, clearly their lawyers having correctly passed the attitude test. A couple more visits were made by the QC to the Court Office. I would have loved to have heard what was being said out there.

Approaching morning adjournment; with mission accomplished there was a meeting of the eyes again between Registrar and Prosecutor, and with the assistance once more of David Copperfield, the court file for the

QC's client, mysteriously reappeared. Those damned pieces of paper sometimes get stuck together with another file, what a crying shame that was! Truth be known, no one really knows how that court file got to be mixed up with the hundred or so files being handled by the Prosecutor. These things just happen, no one is to blame; so, after apologies all-round, the QC's work was done and he headed for the door, to ooze his brand of arrogance elsewhere. It could only have been better if a group of Court Staff and Prosecutors were present to wave as he departed in his Corporate Cab, "Don't you dare darken our doors again, you prized twat".

9. I'M NOT GETTING INTO A SCRAP WITH HIM!

I was running defended hearings one afternoon, upstairs in Courtroom 2 of the Otahuhu District Court. Judge Bouchier was on the bench. She was always good to appear in front of. I had known her since she was a duty solicitor, and when I attended court for defended hearings, as a young Constable. She was also married to a former senior Police Officer, now turned barrister. That certainly gave her an awareness of what the world was really about.

I was partway through examining a witness, when an almighty crash was heard from somewhere outside of the courtroom. The thing about being a Sergeant Prosecutor was that, in an instant you could be required to become a regular Officer, usually for outbreaks of disorder. Of course, there is no such expectation made of civilian barristers. It actually got to the stage, years later that some Judges would not sit, if they did not have a Sergeant Prosecutor in court, or at least some other security cover. It was not uncommon for a defendant to play up, and for the Prosecutor to spring into action to assist an Escort Officer. Sometimes the public gallery would also erupt into abuse, and become violent if the result didn't go their way.

The noise certainly indicated to me that something pretty serious had occurred, but interestingly, there was no follow through of related clatter so I was fairly confident that there wasn't a riot occurring just outside of the courtroom door. The Judge simply looked at me and uttered "Go". I strode purposefully to the door, remembering the words of advice given to me as a young Constable, "Run to a fire, walk to a fight". I exited the courtroom and entered the upstairs foyer. There was no one in the foyer, however a net curtain was flapping wildly against the far wall. I immediately thought that someone had gone through the window, but a closer examination showed that it was intact. I glanced over the railing and looked down towards the ground floor. There was no sign of a body, so the plot was beginning to thicken. I was joined by a colleague who had come from Courtroom 3. Obviously, the problem was not in the upper level so we both headed downstairs.

We were met at the front door of the court by one of the Registrars. We were to become the posse of three. The reinforced lower panel of the front door to the Courthouse was smashed, so that explained the noise that we heard. The Registrar must have attended Boy Scouts as a youngster because he found a blood trail that started small, but was growing with every drop. We headed down the path and up to Prince's Street. We crossed to the other side of the road, and took a turn to the right towards Great South Road. The trail was large and fresh as it headed across Great South Road, and then left towards Station Road. By this stage we were following small pools of blood a short stride apart. We went right into Station Road and past Chris Field's Law Office. Just up ahead on the right was the White Cross Medical Office. As we approached, we could hear the yelling and cursing long before we could see anyone. It was clear that we were closing in on our prey.

As we entered the medical offices, a staff member directed us to a curtained cubicle to the right. Whoever was in there wasn't a happy camper. We opened the curtain and the sight that confronted us was pretty impressive. A rather large Polynesian male was lying on the bench. The floor of the cubicle was almost completely covered in blood, probably as much spilled blood that I had ever seen. The guy attempted a small lunge at us, but his will to take us on was diminishing. Just to make sure, I told the other two members of our posse, that I wasn't going to get into a scrap with this guy. Rolling around in copious amounts of blood, just wasn't what I had planned for that day. I think the medical staff must have been able to pump something into him, because the guy settled down quite quickly, much to our relief. He was wearing shorts so his injury was visible, and serious attempts were being made to stem the blood flow.

We were able to establish that this guy had appeared in the List Court, and was unhappy with the fine imposed upon him. On the way out he kicked the exit door panel in a fit of rage, and basically sliced off his calf muscle. However, he did have the sense to get himself to the Medical Centre. I'm not sure if you can bleed out from a leg wound, but this guy gave it a pretty good go. Top marks to the Court

Registrar for locating the initial blood spots, and helping us to track the quarry. A 'Police Five' badge was probably well deserved. After having the offender taken off our hands by an Incident Patrol, all of us were able to head back to normal duties, after this thirty-minute recess. As I recall, I believe the Judge saw fit to dismiss my case after we had resumed, perhaps it would have been more satisfying if I had stayed and had a scrap instead.

9   Otahuhu Prosecutions Office 2000.

10. RUN, PROSECUTOR, RUN!

Workload was always an issue and ways of managing it were always being looked at. The List Courts were always problematic and difficult to control, because the ever-increasing number of arrests had to be dealt with somewhere. The size of the Judicial List was able to be offset, by a number of the police bailed defendants being further remanded by a Registrar. Such remands didn't generally require a Judge to be involved, although on rare occasions there were disputed issues requiring judicial intervention. The situation was to be improved further with the introduction of Community Magistrates to deal with minor cases, but this was still some years away.

It was decided by Police Prosecutions that the workload of the List Court was too much for one Prosecutor to handle. Rather than having two Prosecutors in place for the entire court sitting, the compromise was to have a morning Prosecutor and an afternoon Prosecutor. This enabled the morning Prosecutor to clear their paperwork in the afternoon, and the afternoon Prosecutor had the opportunity to do so the next morning. One afternoon, I was rostered as the Prosecutor in the List Court at the Otahuhu District Court. An immediate problem was that all of the files listed for hearing, were being seen for the first time. There was an expectation that if some issue had arisen in the morning session, and the case had been set down for the afternoon, then you would receive some sort of briefing about the matter. Some Prosecutors were better at this than others.

On this occasion about three or four cases in, a young guy about twenty, was called up from custody to be sentenced. A number of things began to conspire against me. The docks in District Courts in those days seem to have been designed for appearance rather than security. The dock in Courtroom 1 at Otahuhu was a rectangular enclosure leading from the door to the cell area. It was just over waist height all round. This defendant headed in and positioned himself at the far end of the rectangle. This meant that he was situated just past the Prosecutor's bench, making him closer to the door than me. The Escort Officer was between the defendant and the cell area door. In my opinion this was wrong, and that I believed that he should have positioned himself, so that he was closest to the door. However, I can't really be too critical because the Escort Officer was likely more concerned with being closer to the Judge, than the defendant. It was just poor design all round. I was in the Papakura District Court on one occasion when a defendant mounted the dock and attempted to leap onto the Judges' bench; thankfully falling just short. The design actually encouraged that to happen.

As the Judge heard from the defendant's lawyer I began to flick through the defendant's file. As I got part way through the arrest report, I began to get an uneasy feeling. Apparently, the defendant had a predilection to run whenever possible, and this was a recurring theme throughout the file. I looked over at the defendant and our eyes met. No, it wasn't love at first sight. He knew, that I knew, that he was going to have a go. The Escort Officer was completely oblivious to this developing situation. In hindsight, I should have jumped up, and taken a position between the door and the defendant, and directed the Escort Officer into what I believed to be the correct position. Unfortunately, I didn't do so and the rest is history, although at least I do have this story to tell. A couple more glances and things were getting pretty tense.

Next minute, the defendant vaulted the dock and was heading for the door. I launched myself into action, chair sprawled in the process. As I recall, the Escort Officer was almost asleep at this point, so it was up to me. I always found chasing suspects in police uniform to be quite difficult. I had come from a running background, being quite handy as an 800-metre runner at high school. Nowadays I was more suited to marathons, but I was no slouch. However, trousers and dress shoes weighed down by appointments takes its toll. The young guy was in shorts and trainers, so it was not a fair contest. He was out of the courtroom door before I got up a head of steam. A couple of his supporters were near the doorway and put in a bit of interference. Through the waiting room and out through the court doorway that was damaged in the last chapter. The guy was still in my sights but I wasn't closing him down. As I got to Prince's Street he was already across. I then encountered one of those slow-motion moments, when your senses go into overdrive. I was aware that a large truck was approaching from my left. I knew that if I stopped for it, the offender was gone. A flurry of mental arithmetic produced the answer that I could make it……. just. Calculations proved to be accurate and I made it …. just. Still not gaining but hallelujah, I saw a Constable walking towards me. He must have seen me and the offender and made one of those react as you see it decisions, and decked the guy cold. It took me a couple of moments to get enough breath to thank the cop, and the offender was wheeled off to the cells. I headed back to the courtroom and regained my seat. I made a mental note that something had to be done about the height of the docks, just as the Escort Officer awoke.

In terms of real running, I was always grateful for the assistance I received from the Police Council of Sport (now known as Police Sport). The $2.50 per fortnight subscription gave tremendous value over the years. I ran in quite a number of 'John Clare Memorial' races, travelled to Wellington and Christchurch for the Police Triathlon Championships and went to Melbourne for the 2014 Australasian Police and Emergency Services Games. I was very appreciative of a donation made when I competed in the Paris and London Marathons of 2015. I was very proud to wear their logo printed on the sleeve of my running shirt. I really came into my own when I became aware that Police Sport were trendsetting in the manner in which they held the annual Cross-Country event. It doesn't take a rocket scientist to know that athletic performance is influenced by three factors namely, gender, age and build. Mainstream athletics only acknowledge the existence of gender and age, in the events that they schedule. Police Sport agreed that build was also important and created a draught horse category for male athletes weighing over 95 kilograms. This also recognises that many male Police Officers are on the larger side, some would say for good reason.

I headed down to Paraparaumu in 2009 and managed a second place in the draught horse category. I lost out quite easily to a guy from Hastings who, despite being taller and heavier than me, was about ten years younger. The next year the event was at Te Awamutu and I won in the absence of the Hastings Officer. He did turn up the following year to his home event, and I was second again by quite a distance. Next up was Whanganui, and with no appearance from my nemesis I won for the second time. My third victory was at Palmerston North the following year, and I gained the impression that he might have retired from competition. There was a break for a year before an event was held at Taupo. Another bigger but fitter athlete took over the mantle, and I had to settle for second again. My final outing was in 2017 when the event was held as part of the Police Winter Games at Rotorua. Neither of the guns turned up, so I was able to record my fourth victory. It's quite satisfying in a way to think that my name is engraved four times on a trophy that is held in some dark office somewhere, for time immemorial.

One interesting dilemma that I encountered when I became quite intense about this event, was about weight v performance. Ordinarily I could weigh in at 96 kg pretty easily. The problem being, that the harder I trained the more weight I lost, so I could be around 93 kg about three weeks before the event and would have to bulk up on meal replacement sachets on top of normal meals. Unfortunately, quick weight gain does affect performance. Such is the lot of a thoroughbred…erh… draughthorse, I guess.

10 Police Cross Country Te Awamutu 2010.

11 On the way to my first draughthorse title.

12 Presented with the trophy that would find its way home with me on four occasions.

11. DID IT HURT?

The intellect of some of the Judges that I encountered was truly amazing. Whether it be through a photographic memory, or possession of a large hard drive, some of the legal artistry performed, was a joy to behold. One Judge so blessed, was affectionately known by us as Uncle Lindsay. He possessed not just an incredible legal mind, but his knowledge of people, places and stuff generally, was unrivalled. On one occasion at Papakura, he was dealing with a defendant who had been arrested by Police for disqualified driving in Rotorua. For no particular reason, the Judge then went on to give detailed directions from the scene of the offence to the Rotorua Police Station.

On another occasion, we were trying to strike up some bail terms for a defendant, but he was having difficulty with the specifics for a rural address near Whakatane. After a few questions from Uncle Lindsay, the Judge was able to extract a couple of extended family names from the defendant, and then went on to describe the home the defendant was hoping to be bailed to, including the colour of the rural mail box.

On occasions, some of us believed that he slept through most court proceedings, but clearly that must have been how he pondered problems best, with eyes closed, because he would spring back to life at a moment's notice.

It was no surprise then, that Uncle Lindsay was appointed to hear what was believed to be the first case in our District, involving the illicit possession of a Taser. Some may call it a test case, but that is a term bandied about far too often for my liking, usually by the media. Suffice to say, that we were taking this case seriously. The Detective involved in the case had performed a great job behind the scenes, and the suspect item had been studiously examined by a number of experts. The charge was denied by the defendant, largely to see how things went, in essence putting the Prosecution to the proof.

It was accepted by the defence that the defendant was in possession of the item, so the Judge was only required to find, whether it was an offensive weapon or not. The legal definition required, that we prove that the item was made for causing bodily injury.

The first witness was a scientist from the ESR. His report was long and detailed containing supporting graphs and diagrams. The problem was, that I couldn't understand most of it. I only got 53% for School Certificate Physics, so we weren't off to an encouraging start. The only consolation was, I suspected that the lawyer knew even less than me. I began leading the scientist through the report, when Uncle Lindsay decided that this was a job for a real man, and took over the job.

For about forty-five minutes Uncle Lindsay and the scientist traded comments and explanations with lots of nodding, and the odd chuckle or two. The lawyer and I just grinned at each other, feeling a little like spare ones at a wedding, as the science just swept over us. After the other two had completed their discussion using the longest words and best turn of phrase possible, I was asked to call my next witness.

In walked a cardiologist from Middlemore Hospital. Looking like he would rather be elbow deep in someone's chest, he entered the witness box. He then gave his opinion about the device he had been asked to examine, and in particular, and importantly for our case, what it might do to a human. Uncle Lindsay wanted to ramp things up a bit so asked the Cardiologist "But how do you know?" The Cardiologist was starting to squirm a bit and definitely wanted to be someplace else. "Well there's a bit of a story Your Honour" was his retort. Uncle Lindsay smiled knowingly and replied "I thought that there might be". The Cardiologist then went on to explain what had happened. He claimed that his examination of the device could only produce a theoretical result, and that he wasn't happy with that. He said that he asked one of his senior colleagues to be present and bare witness, and also provide medical assistance if necessary. Making sure that all sorts of medical equipment was at hand, the Cardiologist said that he zapped himself with the device. "Did it hurt?" said Uncle Lindsay. 'By Christ Your Honour, it hurt like hell. I won't be doing that again".

The defence were feeling a little sheepish, and almost changed their plea then and there. Just for completeness though, Uncle Lindsay did what he did best and gave a water tight decision, confirming that based on the abundance of evidence placed before him, it proved that the suspect item was indeed an offensive weapon, and the defendant was duly convicted.

As the court adjourned, I noted Uncle Lindsay giving a longing glance at the Taser. I wondered to myself if he snuck back into the courtroom after we had left, to give it a go for himself?

12. CAN YOU HUM IT FOR ME PLEASE SARGE?

The Otahuhu District Court had long been described as being disorganised and shambolic. I didn't help in this regard. When I was at Papakura, we had a devil of a job getting court files transferred in from Otahuhu. I regret it now, but one day I was asked by the Judge how long a case should be adjourned, for a file to arrive from Otahuhu. Somewhat flippantly, but still deserving quite a laugh, I explained that they were probably thrown out of the office window, and it may take some time to be blown along the Southern Motorway. "Let's give it three weeks then" I suggested. In reality my attitude to them was very harsh. The Otahuhu District Court serviced a high-volume crime area. The staff were committed to the cause, but there simply wasn't enough of them to do the job as efficiently as others expected. I had been told by lawyers about other courts in the Auckland region, that were far worse, so it wasn't all bad.

Despite this, a hotshot Judge from Wellington, signalled that he was on his way to sort out this mess of a court, and he wasn't going to take any prisoners. We had seen this guy previously. No one had anything particularly nice to say about him, so it had all the hallmarks of a perfect storm. He arrived and commenced proceedings by dealing to the local Court Managers. Next step was to sit in a variety of different courtrooms and by God, things were going to proceed smoothly. Each day, reports were received back from our Prosecutors, who had the misfortune to be appearing before him. It was carnage out there, and all anyone wanted was for him to scuttle his way back to Wellington, and be done with it.

Word was received, that he would be doing defended hearings on the Friday. I quickly arranged for a roster change, demanding to have a crack at this piece of work. The morning session commenced, as he meant to go on. The lawyers took a few hits for their sloppy work. I was disappointed to see the Registrar take a couple of swipes also. Certainly not nice, and a definite no-no. He threw a couple of salvos my way, but I was steeled with the resolve that, of course, having been trained by Judge Richardson, there was nothing that this interloper could do, that hadn't already been done before. After the morning session, everyone headed off for sustenance hoping to address their wounds over the break.

A drink drive defended hearing was scheduled for the afternoon. This case was being heard during the bad old days for prosecuting such cases. There was one technical defence after another. It was almost as though parliament didn't want to do anything about the carnage being caused by drunk drivers on our roads. We had all heard of the situation in Victoria, Australia, where all that was required to be proven, was that the defendant was the person driving or attempting to drive and that the level, whether it be breath or blood, was over the limit. We could only dream of such a regime. Even years later when the

Supreme Court specifically decreed that it had enough of technical issues of little merit, in the case of Aylwin v Police,[2] some District Court Judges did their best not to follow it. It really did make you ask whether there was a larger picture somewhere, that only a chosen few had access to. I really felt for the Officers conducting the checkpoints and other vehicles stops. The drink drive procedure was complicated, and quite linear, so that certain doors in the process didn't open until others had been closed. The Department had done its best with a progression of checklists for the Officers to complete. Our view, was that they should be routinely available for the Officers to refer to in court. Defence Counsel were keenly against this, and preferred the situation to be a memory test, for an occurrence that had happened several months earlier. All we could do was to encourage Officers to be careful and make comprehensive and legible notes, and we would help out as best we could, and when permitted to do so by the Judge. The whole unfortunate situation had cultivated a scourge of specialist drink drive lawyers who were certainly good at their craft. Some defendants were prepared to pay many thousands of dollars to these limpets, to avoid being convicted, and therefore disqualified from driving. One thought that I floated, but never received any traction from, was for first time drink drivers under a moderate level, without any other errant driving, to be fined but not disqualified. I am sure that this would have taken away some of the business from the specialists, without the defendant putting their livelihood

---

[2] Aylwin v New Zealand Police NZSC 113 SC 33/2008

at risk or face further expense for a limited licence application. Call me old fashioned, but surely the initial wakeup call, without mandatory disqualification, would put most people back on the straight and narrow.

On this afternoon we began okay, but the Defence Counsel was starting to make some progress with the inexperienced young constable, who just wanted to get back out on the street, and start locking some people up again. The evidence concluded, and I knew that it was probably a lost cause, but the Judge wanted it spelt out in words of one syllable, so he asked Counsel for submissions. The lawyer was able to highlight three issues, which he considered were fatal to the prosecution case. It wasn't really a surprise to me, because I wasn't a stranger to these types of cases. The Judge looked down at me in an all-knowing and condescending manner; keen to hear my response. I quickly addressed the first two points, and the glance from the Judge indicated that I was on the right track. Having put the first two issues to bed, I took on the third, which I already knew to be a bit of a problem. I waxed on for a bit, trying my best but it just wasn't coming together. The Judge finally stepped in and proclaimed that I had done pretty well with the first two, but the third issue was terminal. I took a deep breath and determined that it was time to take one for the team. This Judge had been giving all of us grief for the better part of the week, and I wanted to change the mood somewhat. I then came out with the best legal submission I ever made. "Your Honour I ask that you consider the immortal words of Meat Loaf, who quite correctly and concisely, stated that 'Two Out of Three Ain't Bad!'." Now at this point I thought that I had probably done enough to see the inside of a cell, but the Judge laughed, quite raucously I might add. However, he proclaimed that "It might be good enough for Meat Loaf, Sergeant, but it's not going to work in my court".

I know that some of you are looking at the title of this story and are starting to wonder, but alas, no he didn't utter those words. It would really have made my day if he did.

13. HOW MANY ZEROS WAS THAT?

Peter Benjamin Lewis flew to New Zealand in January 2000, ostensibly to view the Americas' Cup yacht racing. He was the chairman of Progressive Insurance Company in the USA, and despite being a billionaire he was relatively unassuming. The problem for him though, was that he was a drug user. The reason given by him, was that it provided some form of pain relief for a partial amputation of his leg. Matters started to unravel for Mr Lewis when he was apprehended at Auckland International Airport, in possession of cannabis plant and resin. When Police became aware that his super yacht was already berthed at the Viaduct Harbour, the Auckland Drug Squad got involved and executed a search warrant on it. Some more cannabis plant and resin were located, and Lewis was arrested and charged at the Otahuhu Police Station. One of my soon to be prosecution colleagues, later advised me that he had been the Custody Sergeant when Lewis was brought in. Lewis did indeed bunk it rough in the flea pit that the Otahuhu cells were quickly becoming. The only allowance was, that he was able to order in his own food, as the local variety was found to be not overly palatable. There was no additional expense to the taxpayer; it could be argued that there was a slight saving.

After what I presume was a peaceful night's rest at 'Club Med Otahuhu', Lewis was being readied for his court appearance at the equally hospitable, Otahuhu District Court, helpfully just next door. What needs to be remembered is, that this was during the 'holiday' period for the court. Not an excuse, just a reality. I was first to arrive at the office, being rostered for List Court. From memory, our total staff for the day was probably two Prosecutors and a Support Officer. I was met at the door by Lewis' lawyer, a very experienced operator I had dealt with often over the years. She had certainly come prepared; I'm guessing after being quite well remunerated. She explained the situation to me and presented a weighty document that went into Lewis' corporate background, and an overview of his philanthropic work. I spent some time going over the papers, which were fairly impressive. Lewis had made donations of well over 100 million dollars over the years, including funds for a library at Princeton University and stake money for the Guggenheim Museum. I was advised that Lewis was a self-confessed drug user to assist with pain relief. The explanation to be given to the court, was that he had brought his own supply with him from the States, rather than becoming involved in the New Zealand drug industry.

Counsel advised that she would be seeking a discharge without conviction for Lewis, due to the impact a conviction would have upon his business interests, and the ability to travel. This case was dealt with under s.19 Criminal Justice Act 1985. The Sentencing Act 2002 had not yet arrived; however, the principle was largely the same. Do the consequences of a conviction outweigh the seriousness of the offending? At this time, it was quite rare for written submissions to be prepared for the court, matters were pretty much dealt with on the fly. I must say that times have changed in that regard, to the extent that the amount of time spent now by both parties on written legal submissions, is quite frankly, absurd. Counsel advised that Lewis would be prepared to make a charitable donation in lieu of a fine, if he were to be discharged without conviction. This in itself was not unusual, but was not mandatory for such cases. What was unusual was the amount of the donation. Lewis was prepared to donate the sum of $50 000 to Odyssey House, the major Auckland Drug Rehabilitation Centre, that interestingly operates with limited Government funding, and requires external donations to survive. The usual charitable donation linked to a discharge without conviction was around $500. Her argument was that a more substantial donation would more adequately reflect the means of Lewis. Was it too much? It appears so, the shit storm that was to come, seemed to indicate that people thought that Lewis should pay what everyone else does.

I thanked the lawyer for her efforts and told her that I would give the matter some thought. I rang the Drug Squad Detective Senior Sergeant, who advised that there were no suggestions of the defendant dealing in drugs, and that there was nothing to negate Lewis' explanation. He wasn't seen as a major target and no objection was raised to the prospect of a discharge without conviction being granted. I completed my assessment and met the lawyer over at court. I advised that the prosecution would raise no objection, but suggested that we should run the proposal past the Judge. If he was not on board, then I had told Counsel that I would opt out, and that she would have to convince the Judge on her own. She was happy with that. As it turned out the Judge quickly came up to speed with the situation, and determined that the proposal would be an appropriate outcome. The defendant was then remanded overnight on bail to make the arrangements. 'Club Med Otahuhu' was just becoming a particularly bad memory.

Overnight the jungle drums started to beat out loud. Some 'rich yank' down South Auckland way was trying to buy himself some justice, and the media were determined that was not going to happen. The court was packed to overflowing the next morning; the press having answered the call to another "Constable on Indecent Assault" situation, but this time it was real. You could almost sense the hostility, "How dare this yank save our cash strapped drug rehab centre from insolvency. He can rot in prison with those other drug dealing scumbags for all we care!"

What I don't believe was ever reported about this day, was what occurred about three cases before Lewis was dealt with. As chance would have it another American, down-under on holiday, had also been caught at the airport with some cannabis plant. There was no fancy lawyer for this guy. He too must have been keen to check out of 'Club Med Otahuhu', and he was pleading guilty, via one of our own tax payer funded Duty Solicitors. The Judge wanted to know a bit more about this guy, who was described as a civil servant. Just what did he do to serve the good folk of the U S of A? He explained that his role was akin to our own Health and Safety officials. The Judge asked what would become of his job when his employer found out about a conviction for possessing cannabis. The defendant said that he would end up on welfare. Now it might well be argued that a Health and Safety assessor, shouldn't be blinded by the effects of cannabis whilst testing out safety rails, and the like, but nonetheless it was within the Judge's prerogative to offer a discharge without conviction. Having a somewhat lighter wallet than Lewis, this was going to be dealt with by a $500 charitable donation. As I recall, but of course do stand to be corrected, this case didn't make the pages of any of our dailies. No, of course not, everyone was there for the main event.

Lewis was called to the dock and his Counsel presented the receipt for the charitable donation made to Odyssey House, and passed on that they were exceedingly grateful. There was some talk of the Centre being added to Lewis' annual donation list, but that was something that he would give further consideration to, when back in the States (*in actuality this never occurred probably due to the events that followed*). The Judge spoke with Lewis for a short while. All that seemed to be reported was the parting pleasantry "Go now and enjoy yourself in our fine city". Nothing about the lecture, highlighting Lewis' stupidity in bringing drugs to New Zealand when he was entrusted to make sound decisions impacting on many lives, and sizeable amounts of money on a daily basis, in his business life. Where matters did go astray though, was right at the end. The discharge without conviction was granted. As Lewis left the dock his lawyer, almost as an afterthought it appeared to me, rose to her feet and uttered the words

"Name suppression, Your Honour?" The Judge then granted name suppression.

Well by this time, the gathered media were almost foaming at the mouth, seeing their opportunity to have a crack at this tall poppy from the States beginning to disappear from view. The days and weeks that followed focussed initially upon the idea of justice being bought, but that began to fade when it actually did stack up in terms of legal precedents. However, the name suppression issue, which the Prosecution didn't give a toss about, took upon a life of its own. At the end of the road it transpired from the Court of Appeal that the granting of name suppression itself, was not really the problem. The issue as they saw it, was that no reasoning had been given for the decision. This case provided impetus for legislative change that required full reasons to be given relating to all decisions made by the courts.

As for me, how did I fair? A quick chat with the National Manager, who was content with my actions, and I was back to fight another day. In case anyone is wondering, no, I don't have a hidden Swiss bank account bulging in US dollars.

P.S. I'm just back from a trip to the US which included a visit to the Guggenheim Museum in New York. I was pleased to note that a theatre or is that theater, on the lower level was named after Mr Lewis. At least his stated philanthropic deeds appear to have been genuine.

13 An interesting find at the Guggenheim Museum.

14. DOES ANYONE HERE DRIVE LEGALLY SARGE?

Even though we had locally based Judges, there was always rostering difficulties, and it was not unusual to appear in front of a visiting Judge from elsewhere in the country. The benefit of appearing in front of Judges that you knew, was that you could adapt your style depending upon who was on the bench. Sometimes pushing the correct button, at just the right moment could bring the desired result. Likewise, if you knew that you were appearing in front of certain Judges, you left some tricks in the office.

It was fair to assume that visiting Judges sentenced heavier, and generally had a low regard for the standard of justice being dispensed in South Auckland. This probably smacks a bit of parochialism, and as a result of some horror stories told to them by other judicial colleagues. One time I appeared before a South Islander, in what I considered was a fairly routine morning in a List Court. When I arrived back in court after lunch, the Registrar told me that the Judge wanted to see me in Chambers. Things had gone pretty well I thought, so I was slightly apprehensive about this meeting. As it transpired, I shouldn't have been concerned. The Judge was simply doing his due diligence, and asked me if his sentencing was in accordance with what I expected. In particular, he was concerned about the number of defendants appearing before him charged with driving with excess breath/ blood alcohol, and driving whilst disqualified. I assured him that his sentencing was fair and he finished our meeting by commenting, "Does anyone here drive legally Sarge?"

Another time, I ended up with a split defended hearing court before a Judge from the deep south. These split courts were the bane of our existence. Generally, a single Prosecutor had prepared the files scheduled for defended hearing, and made any necessary adjustments with the Officer in Charge of the case. That Prosecutor would then attend the start of the court hearing, when the cases were called through, to see what was going to happen. No one can blame the court for assigning more cases than actual hearing time as the attrition rate, despite efforts to address it, has always been high. There are always late changes of plea to guilty. There are often adjournments sought by either party, for a multitude of reasons. Sometimes the Prosecution folds late, due to a lack of witnesses or realisation that the case just wasn't going to make the grade. Some days the cases that are ready to proceed to defended hearing fit comfortably within the available hearing time; on occasions nothing proceeding to an evidential hearing. More often than not though, the number of cases needing to be heard is greater than the capability of one Judge. That is when the court hierarchy springs into action. If a spare Judge can be located (as their allocated business has been completed), then a court taker is located, a spare courtroom identified and the prosecution is advised to find a Prosecutor. This is not something that appellate courts would find acceptable for Defence Counsel, being required to pick up and run with a case at very short notice. However, it was generally expected by most Judges, that Prosecutors could take on a case with only a few minutes preparation, and it happened all the time. Those of us with a bit of experience under our belts would actually relish these splits and come free from other duties to "help out", what in reality was a poorly organised and overburdened case scheduling system. For more junior Prosecutors, who preferred to know a case backwards, these splits were something to be loathed. It was not uncommon to turn up and have the split Judge ask, "Are you ready Sarge?", 'I've had 10 minutes to look at the file, Your Honour so I guess so", "Well, then let's learn this one together, shall we?"

A really bizarre situation arose on one of these days when I was handed a split defended hearing at the Otahuhu District Court. The Judge was visiting from out of town, and was therefore an unknown quantity to me. The case had originally been scheduled in the main court building on Princes Street. However, when the split occurred, we were assigned to one of the secondary courtrooms on Albion Road. The Officer in Charge of the case had explained to me that his complainant was on standby, but he had given her a call and she was on her way. As a Prosecutor, I didn't really mind allowing witnesses to be on standby. Hell, the court system stuffs up the plans of so many people that if we could, in a small way accommodate them, then it was a risk worth taking. A risk certainly, as the court day can change rapidly, and you could be caught short if you didn't adapt promptly enough.

However, the standby system mostly worked well, and in fact quite a few witnesses on standby never got the call to come in.

The Judge was keen to get on with things, and he understood that our complainant was on the way, so I called the case out of order with the young Constable to give evidence first. Initially things proceeded normally, but halfway through his evidence in chief, a mobile phone began to ring. This was the early days of mobile phones and very few people carried them. I certainly didn't have one and it was many years before they were issued by the Police Department to all staff.

I had certainly been in court when one had gone off in the public gallery. Once, the Judge would tolerate it, twice not so much so. It was even better when Defence Counsel were caught out by their phone going off whilst they were in the courtroom. One Counsel had it down pat though; as he would point at others, whilst everyone knew that the ringing was coming from his bag. Another urban legend was that when Court Escort staff were feeling a little bored, they would notify the downstairs Control Room as to which lawyers were in the courtroom, and phone calls on a blocked number would be made to the lawyers in court, to see if they were on silent or not. Occasionally some stupid member of the public would feel the need to take a photo of the Judge from the public gallery. Once I was present when a Judge identified just that, and the phone was seized. The Judge hovered over the 'delete all' button in this idiot's photo library for quite some time, before contenting himself with just deleting the offending photo.

However, this was the first occasion, I or indeed upon further investigation, any Prosecutor, had a Constable receive a phone call whilst in the witness box and giving evidence. It didn't stop there though, **he answered it!** A million thoughts were going through my head, and I happened to look at the Judge who said, "I'll take care of this Sarge". I was pretty pleased about this, because I didn't really know what I was going to say. To his credit the Judge was fairly calm about it, far more so than I was feeling. The back story though, was that the complainant had turned up at the main court building, and couldn't find the courtroom. She then rang the Constable, who happened to be in the witness box, and he thought that it was her, so decided that it would be a good idea to answer it. That's generation Y, I suppose. Nonetheless, I dined out on that story for years to come.

15. EVERYTHING IS ROSY?

What can be done about family violence? It's always been a problem, and despite huge efforts over the years, and a truck load of funding, it is still a problem. If anything, reported family violence statistically, is on the increase, as victims and witnesses respond to the call to 'Speak Out'. The concept of the cycle of violence, whereby a parent passes on poor social behaviour to their offspring is well reported. Historically, the criminal justice system has not served family violence at all well. The criminal law is all about proof, rather than the truth. Sometimes these two concepts co-exist, but often they don't.

The criminal law also contains an age-old principle, whereby the defendant is entitled to confront their accuser. Quite a problem, when it involves persons in an intimate relationship, often separated by bail conditions, airing their differences in a courtroom, something like six months later. Worse than that, the court process only allows closed courts for certain types of cases, and family violence is not one of them. Therefore, the complainant must recount their version of events, and stand up to the rigours of cross examination, not only in front of their partner, but also any member of the public who decides to turn up, to catch up with the gossip. A former Chief District Court Judge once said, that if you couldn't get a complainant in a family violence case into court and giving evidence within six weeks of the incident, then you could expect that witness to recant. Unsurprisingly, the courts are not particularly proactive regarding short time frames. It certainly could not be said in the world of family violence, that 'everything is rosy'.

That is not to say that advancements haven't been made to attempt to improve the court process. When I was first prosecuting family violence cases, spousal privilege was able to be claimed by legally married persons. In essence the witness was called to the witness box and the Prosecutor would establish the nature of the relationship, including the when and where of their marriage. The witness would then be advised that they didn't have to give evidence against their partner, unless they chose to do so. Many would opt out at that point, and the Prosecutor would be asked by the Judge whether there was any other evidence. Often there wasn't, and the charge would be dismissed. What did I tell you, proof versus truth? On the occasions that a witness did not claim spousal privilege, it was a pretty good indicator that they were keen to tell the truth. Not always though. Even a witness who didn't claim spousal privilege may attempt to take the blame themselves, or seriously minimise the involvement of the defendant. Spousal privilege was removed with the passing of the Evidence Act 2006.

My strategy with family violence cases was to try to achieve some sort of result. That might mean a reduction in charge, or watering down of the summary of facts. What I wanted was, either a guilty plea or the defendant being found guilty of.... something. A finding of guilt meant that the Judge could actually do something to address the underlying issue. The worst result for me was a defendant walking out of court scot free, often wearing a smirk, thinking that they could get away with violence towards their partner. On many occasions the system would provide such a poor and unsatisfactory experience for the complainant, that they would choose not to report any future transgressions. This might be great news for the workload of the court but not ideal for many victims.

One idea that I had, but it will never receive any traction, is that lower level family violence cases, probably involving a first timer, should be dealt with outside of the standard criminal justice process. It would require a changed legislative framework, but such cases would fall somewhere between the Family Court and the District Court. There would be a presumption that the complained of incident actually occurred. Therefore, from the first court appearance, efforts could be made to address the issues and processes such as rehabilitation and counselling could begin. No one would be required to give evidence, and there would be no undue time delays. Defendants who complied and made progress to the satisfaction of the court, would be dealt with appropriately by the Judge. This might involve a discharge without conviction, amongst other sanctions. Poor performance would result in tougher action by the court.

One of the earliest family violence defended hearings I prosecuted was at the Papakura District Court. I recognised a variation of a defendant's name amongst the files, when I was preparing them the day before hearing. I made a few enquiries to confirm my suspicions and then sat back to see how it played out. The presiding Judge had the reputation of being defence friendly, although I did get on with her quite well. On the day most of the cases were sorted out in one way or another, and I was fizzing with anticipation when the defendant was called up in the case in which I now had something up my sleeve. The hearing commenced in a conventional manner, with the complainant giving evidence as expected. Under cross examination it became apparent from the line of questioning by his lawyer that the defendant was going to run a self defence argument. Here is where things got a little interesting. The complainant portrayed as a rather diminutive figure and the defendant was a mountain of a man, albeit slightly past his prime. I could sense that the Judge was intrigued as to how the case was playing out. Not unexpectedly the defendant gave evidence to provide the foundation for his claim of self-defence. Before long, it was my turn to cross examine the defendant. I started slowly by making comment about the defendant's build and fitness, which I contrasted against the size of the complainant. The defence lawyer was still quite smug at this stage, but just about choked on the pen that he was chewing on when I put the fact to the defendant that he had been the New Zealand Heavyweight Boxing Champion only a few years earlier. The defendant was quite proud of that fact and was more than happy to answer any question I put to him about his illustrious career and in particular the number of knockouts he had achieved. The Judge had almost fallen off the bench at this point and the defence counsel was really wishing that the defendant had opened up a little more to him about his sporting prowess. Suffice to say, the defendant's claim of self-defence crashed and burned shortly afterwards. This case confirmed that the answers aren't always found in the law books.

On occasions, some cases just really annoyed you. One afternoon, a couple were having a violent argument in the car park between Gordon Road and King Street, Otahuhu. It developed to the extent that the female involved was being seriously assaulted. A couple of members of the public noticed this and called for the Police. The Police attended and arrested the male. The members of the public gave a compelling account of what they had seen, and were prepared to give evidence if needed. The victim was uncooperative and maintained that nothing had happened. She was displaying modest facial injuries, which she claimed was as a result of an accidental fall. The defendant pleaded not guilty and a few months later a defended hearing took place. The victim attended with the defendant, and she was offered to the defence as a witness, which was a better tactical option, rather than being called by the Prosecution. The two civilians gave clear, detailed evidence outlining the assault. Neither was shaken from their resolve during cross examination. The defendant said that nothing occurred, as did the victim. The Judge then determined that, he was not prepared to find that the case had been proven beyond a reasonable doubt; completely declining to make a credibility finding. The defendant walked free, offering some words and a glare at the citizens, who had just been doing their duty. Their experience on this occasion likely influenced whether they would become involved in such an incident in the future.

As for the Judge; what was he thinking? Certainly not about trying to make our communities better and safer places.

A few years later at Manukau District Court, I was involved in the mother of all family violence defended hearing court sessions. The full back story was, that I was the Senior Sergeant of Prosecutions, when one of my staff who was rostered for the court, had to go to Australia at short notice for a family issue. I went into the Office on the Sunday before and acquainted myself with the twelve or so cases which had already been properly prepared by the Prosecutor. On the Monday morning, I went over to the court and became aware of which Judge was to be sitting. Now it's fair to say that this Judge and I did not get along. I have no idea what started it, but it was certainly a bit of a problem. The courtroom was unusual, in that the public gallery faced the court side on. I have never encountered any other courtroom set out that way. The day began, and again, for no reason known to me, the Judge and I were at each other like there was no tomorrow. Complainants were being called, spousal privilege claimed, charges dismissed and a number of fiery exchanges between us. This wasn't a Judge Richardson dealing to. It was something more than that, but I wasn't sure what. We got to morning adjournment and I was losing seven nil. After the Judge had left the courtroom, I turned to the gallery and asked the several Constable's present, "Anyone want to be a Prosecutor"? Not surprisingly there were no takers; only words of encouragement for round two that was to begin shortly. I commenced another hearing and called the complainant.

Spousal privilege was unable to be claimed, but without warning, the witness commenced the most violent rant I had ever encountered in a courtroom. I looked over, and confirmed that some backup was still present, because I was concerned that things might get violent. I managed to get a word in and asked the question of the Judge, "Hostile?". "Oh, I don't think so Sergeant!" I just thought to myself that it was going to be a very long day.

The next occasion I was rostered to appear in a List Court before this Judge, I steeled myself and came with a determined attitude for the day to proceed smoothly, at least from my point of view. Within ten minutes we were at each other's throats. I did try to address the issue I was having with this Judge, but my efforts came to nothing. To this day, I still have no idea why we couldn't get along and indeed what was the cause of the issue.

On another occasion, a Judge in the Family Violence Court advised me to tone down my approach to the complainants when they were giving evidence. I was advised that the complainants sitting in the gallery waiting to give evidence were terrified of me. I don't know why, I'm actually of quite a gentle persona. I politely acquiesced, but deep down I knew that I was firmly in the camp of searching for the truth, instead of being content with simply looking for proof. If it meant ruffling a few feathers along the way, then that was the cost of doing business.

At the end of the day I was just trying to make a difference and hopefully influence the future, rather than simply going through the motions. I failed to see why some of the Judges didn't see things like that also.

16. BUT BOSS, THERE'S NO HOLE AT THE BOTTOM OF THE FUNNEL.

Some of the most difficult but also rewarding cases to prosecute related to serious motor vehicle crashes. You will note my use of the word "crash". Some years ago, the Police made a concerted effort to describe these incidents as crashes, rather than accidents. The word "accident" tends to suggest a lack of blame, when in reality a human failing is the cause of most crashes. By adopting a word that indicates blame, it promotes awareness amongst the public, and might in a small way assist with modifying driver behaviour. I still cringe when there are media reports of "accidents" rather than "crashes", and it is clear that they must have missed receiving the memo. One of the real problems with prosecuting serious crashes involving death and/or serious injury, is that most involve an element of carelessness on behalf of the offending driver. That is, the crash and the outcome was never intended to occur, it came about as a result of a driver not reaching the required standard of a reasonable prudent motorist. Therefore, as a general rule, the degree of carelessness is punished by the court rather than the unfortunate outcome. That's why you will have seen the headlines stating that a life was only deemed to be worth 200 hours of Community Work. However, if there is an element of intent involved and the charge relates to a dangerous or reckless act, or an act involving the over consumption of alcohol or drugs, then the gloves are off, and imprisonment is likely.

On the point of alcohol consumption, I do find it strange that our law allows innocent consumption to a certain level, which then becomes unlawful over that level, determined by a breath or blood test. It is well known that the driving population is made up of persons of different ages, gender, build and, metabolism yet the designated level for all adult drivers is the same. On far too many occasions, I have heard Judges in court advise defendants that there is no safe level for alcohol consumption and driving, and that the best practise is not to drink and drive at all. Why then, is that not the law? It's bizarre when you compare this situation to other criminal acts. An assault is the intentional application of force to another. There is nothing there, about how strong the application of force is, that is a matter for sentencing. There is nothing in the definition of theft or fraud to suggest that you haven't committed an offence if you only stole something of limited value. To suggest that you can consume alcohol legally to a certain level with only guess work to determine where that level is, does not address the degree of harm caused within the community. I'm thinking that the alcohol lobby probably has quite a bit to do with this unusual situation.

I have prosecuted a substantial number of cases relating to serious crashes. Initially these crashes were investigated by non-specialist Officers, which lead to the proliferation of hired guns being called by the defence. Most of these people were well qualified, but you couldn't avoid the impression that some of the reports had a slant towards the person footing the bill. This in turn resulted in the Police establishing Serious Crash Units, made of up Officers well trained in all aspects of crash investigation. Often that was enough, but then it became apparent that a suit was being held in higher regard by a Judge than a blue uniform, so on some occasions, serious money was spent to return fire with our own hired gun.

Some of the cases I dealt with were a little unusual. One involved an elderly blind woman who was walking along a residential footpath with her guide dog. The defendant was about twenty metres up his straight driveway, in his van about to reverse out. His teenage daughter was in the front passenger seat. This was always a difficult scenario for the defendant, because there was insufficient room to turn the vehicle around within his property. The roadway itself, was generally too busy for him to reverse up the driveway when entering. Alongside the offside of the driveway, on the border was a large overgrown hedge. In reality he had very little, if any, visibility when crossing over the footpath onto the road at the end of his driveway. However, it is important to note that situation was his problem, not any pedestrian who may be using the footpath. Well you guessed it, he reversed out and struck the elderly pedestrian, the guide dog doing its best to avoid the situation, without success. Despite being seriously injured, the pedestrian did recover and was able to attend court, where the defendant faced a charge of careless use of a motor vehicle causing injury. Our case was based on what the defendant failed to do, bearing in mind that all of the burden of proceeding safely, fell upon him. Firstly, it was stated that something should have been done about the hedge, secondly the daughter should have been dispatched to the end of the driveway to confirm that the way was clear. If she wasn't there, then the defendant himself should have alighted from his vehicle before reaching the crossing to confirm that no one was coming. The defence were calling it an "accident" and that the defendant did all he could in the circumstances. Clearly, they didn't get the memo either. The defence also wanted the evidence of the elderly complainant to be provided to the Judge in a written format, known as "hand up". What people need to know is that, more often than not, the court process needs to be visual rather than blandly recorded on a piece of paper. Suffice to say, there was no way on this earth that I wasn't going to call the complainant. The amount of sympathy our case got when I called her to the witness box, with the guide dog laying down alongside was priceless. It was pretty unlikely that I was going to lose that one. I couldn't resist a bit of a smug glance at Counsel as I observed the result of my handywork.

Some cases just annoy the hell out of you. I didn't prosecute this one, but I was involved in the consultation stage to determine whether a charge should be laid. Some of you might have noticed the white 'In Memoriam' bicycle on Tamaki Drive near Kelly Tarlton's. A motorist had pulled over into a parking space on the side of Tamaki Drive at rush hour one evening. The deceased was cycling along Tamaki Drive approaching the defendant's vehicle. The defendant opened his driver's door; the deceased took an evasive swerve and went under a truck that was alongside. The case related to the actions that were expected from a reasonable prudent motorist in the circumstances. At best, the defendant checked his rear-view mirror and possibly side mirror. There was no mention of looking over his shoulder for a direct view behind him without the use of a mirror (which are subject to blind spots). This was rush hour after all, and there appears to have been no consideration given to sliding over and onto the passenger seat, and exiting the vehicle from the passenger's side. Bearing in mind that the deceased was entirely within their right to cycle unimpeded along the roadway, those actions are the least that the defendant should have done. Suffice to say the Judge saw it differently, and the charge was dismissed, as he found that the defendant did all that was necessary. Heaven help us!

I was sent over to court one afternoon to take on a split court, which meant little preparation time, but the case looked pretty good to me. A motorcyclist was travelling along Chapel Road towards Howick. It was dark and the scientific analysis showed that his headlight was functioning. The defendant was travelling the other way along Chapel Road and turned right into the Botany Town Centre upper carpark in front of the motor-cycle. A collision occurred which saw the vehicle and motor cyclist erupt in flames. Incredibly, and thankfully the motorcyclist survived, and was able to give evidence at trial, although his recollection of the incident was very limited. Now, this case was a stock standard slam dunk. The motor cyclist was travelling in a straight path and had all the rights. The defendant had a legal duty of care to any approaching vehicle, and could not make a turn unless the way was clear. The only slight wriggle room for the defendant would have been if the motorcycle's headlight was not operating, and therefore was unable to be seen. That was not the situation here. We got through about half of the case in the afternoon available. The case was then deemed to be part heard, which is not uncommon. Unfortunately, the Judge transferred to the Auckland District Court shortly afterwards, which complicated the situation a little. A date was set to resume, and hopefully complete the hearing at the Auckland District Court a couple of months later. The evening before that hearing, a specialist report from a defence hired gun arrived. I became aware of it when I met up with members of the Serious Crash Unit at the Auckland District Court, the next morning. By law, there is a requirement for specialist reports to be disclosed to the other party at least ten working days prior to hearing. The defence had failed to do so. Even though our case was quite simple, and on a solid factual basis, this particular hired gun had a reputation and indeed an ability, to have Judges eating from his palm. I therefore rejected service, and the case was further adjourned. That remand was solely due to a defence failure to comply with the law, and there was no criticism of the Prosecution from the bench. I felt it was important that our experts have a proper opportunity to digest the defence report, rather than rushing forward for convenience sake. Unfortunately, that's when things took a turn for the worse. The court were unable to schedule a new hearing date that suited all parties, and a few months later the defence filed for the case to be dismissed for systemic delay. Despite our opposition, and the fact that none of the delay was the fault of the Prosecution, the Judge dismissed the case. What really hurt, was a comment in the Judge's decision that "this is a minor case". A man burst into flames for Christ sake! Sometimes you just wanted to spew. We were really hoping that the victim was going to hit the media with this one, sadly he chose not to.

You might well ask, that if you don't like the result, then why not appeal? That sounds simple and it is, for the defence, who simply file a notice. For the Prosecution, there is one hurdle after another. Initially a comprehensive report outlining the case is required, which is fair enough. However Legal Section wouldn't generally act until a copy of the complained of decision, had been received from the court. Now there are timeframes involved in all of this, and let's just say, it was "difficult" to get a decision released from the court within those time frames. It was almost as though they knew! Anyway, if a miracle did occur, Crown Law had to approve the filing of any Appeal Notice. Generally speaking, a new and unargued area of the law was required or an absolute "mare" of a decision from a Judge. I had seen quite a few of those but they were always toned down to "unusual" or "light". The bottom line was, that very few appeals were commenced on behalf of the Police Prosecution Service. This issue cropped up when the National Manager turned up one day to discuss the findings of our annual culture survey. In the early days the National Manager came to spread the good oil with these reports, over time this reduced to the Area Manager, District Manager and then finally you just got a copy and could talk it over with your boss if you wished. On this occasion though, a direct question was asked of the National Manager about the perceived lack of cases going to appeal. He waxed on for a while in "boss speak" and spoke of a funnel with lots going in the top, and the really good stuff coming out the bottom, but wasn't able to convince anyone. I then piped up, as I did from time to time and said, "But boss, there's no hole at the bottom of the funnel!" I could tell that he was seriously pissed off with me but there were no later repercussions. I guess that he knew the truth after all.

14. Manukau Police Prosecutions Office 2003.

17. LOOKS CAN BE DECEIVING.

Sitting around a courthouse can be a bit dispiriting. You are going to see quite a range of what the community has to offer. Some people are down on their luck; some are career criminals, and some are just there to see what's going on. Each have their stories I suppose. Some have long memories, and attempt to tell you a story of some interaction you had with them, years before. Occasionally, when I was bored on a quiet List Day, I would wait for a defendant to be called to the dock. I'd take a peek at their date of birth and see how they compared to me. I'm not proclaiming to be a particularly fine specimen, but my scientific observation is that crime, drugs and alcohol are not good for your health. We've all seen those progressive mug shots, which commence with an attractive eighteen-year-old and end at age twenty-five with her looking like a haggard old tart, on death's door.

Some criminals though, use their God given gifts to their advantage. I was running a family violence defended hearing against one such guy, and in the end, I felt somewhat inadequate. Despite having half his face covered in tattoos, this guy had the flowing locks, and the swagger to get those women into line. The complainant was in the witness box and I was trying to get something useable from her. They of course, had long since made up so it was near on impossible. So, in the first instance, I had the complainant swooning all over the defendant. I looked up and saw that the female Judge was acting kind of interested also. The female Registrar was also trying to get in on the action. Looking over my shoulder, I could see that the female Defence Counsel was thanking her lucky stars for this assignment, but was kind of resentful of the looks the complainant was giving her guy. Then I noticed the female Court Escort Officer, and she's at it as well. In the end I was wishing for Scotty to beam me up out of there, or at least give me a tutu so I could join the party.

There is a guy who appears from time to time, and he has been described as the country's worst stalker. His problem is that just about any female he encounters, will provide him with a fixation that can only turn out badly. It could possibly be said, that he's stalked more women than he's had hot dinners. Quite a sad story in a way, because this is a diagnosed medical condition, but the system prefers to deal with him, by locking him up rather than addressing the medical issue, if that is even possible. Whenever he appears in court, the powers that be make arrangements so that only males are present, as they are apparently immune from his affliction. Strange but true. Of course, it could be argued that all men suffer from this ailment, to some degree, often depending upon how much alcohol has been consumed.

Sometimes you are in court when notables appear. I was in the Papakura District Court the day Bailey Kurariki, aged twelve years, appeared in relation to the killing of pizza delivery driver Michael Choy. There was an audible gasp when he was led into the courtroom. I couldn't believe what I was seeing. He was such a diminutive, insignificant looking kid. I really wondered what had happened to New Zealand society for it to come to this.

I also witnessed a couple of the early appearances of Antonie Dixon. On the two occasions I saw him, he appeared reasonably normal, or as normal as a drug crazed meth head can be. A while later, I saw a news report of a court appearance, and he had the bizarre bowl haircut and was sporting those goggle eyes that we all came to love. We all knew then, that he was going to have a crack at the insanity route, but in the end, it came to no avail at trial. I'm probably not alone in saying that the world is a much better place without him.

This example reinforces the adage that first impressions can be deceiving. There can be quite a bit of down time during the court day and it can provide an opportunity to chew the fat with lawyers, court staff and other Police Officers. One day I got talking to a new Police Escort Officer, and I was taken back quite a bit with what I saw. This guy had the most visible tattoos that I had seen on any Police Officer and for a moment I wondered if the recruiters had made a mistake. I got talking with him and he was quietly spoken and clearly quite intelligent. I learnt that he was the lead singer of a death metal band. He explained that they had released a couple of successful albums and had toured fairly extensively overseas. I like a broad range of music but I listened to some of this guy's 'crooning' on Spotify and clearly, we were on a different page. Over the weeks and months, I had a number of very entertaining discussions with this officer and concluded that it would be hard to meet a much nicer and genuine guy. He clearly had a good rapport with the prisoners, I'm guessing that the tattoos had something to do with it. From time to time he was the subject of attempts at a 'beat up' by the media. To their credit the Department didn't buy into it and the officer was quoted as saying that "you can't buy that sort of publicity". I was pleased that the media's attempts to discredit the officer gained no traction. One day I was heading back to Court after the lunch break and was approaching the pedestrian crossing at the intersection of Manukau Station Road and Osterley Way. On the other side of the road, I noticed a wheelchair bound defendant who had been involved in quite frequent altercations with Police. He was struggling to make any headway up the incline leading to the Manukau District Court. As luck would have it the Escort Officer was making his way back to Court and he happened across the struggling defendant. A few pleasantries were exchanged and the officer pushed the defendant the 100 metres or so to the entrance of the Court. I must say that my observation of this provided quite a warm feeling inside.

A case that I prosecuted in the twilight of my career really did illustrate how technological advances have changed many aspects of crime detection. When I started with Police, fingerprinting was about as high tech as it got. The advances with assessing DNA evidence, computer-based Intelligence Analysis and CCTV quality and accessibility, have radically changed the landscape. Particularly pleasing, has been the high number of back captured DNA traces, some stretching back decades. I also recall an early case I prosecuted involving CCTV footage. A few minutes in, I asked the investigator when the offence was going to be shown and apparently, I had missed it a minute or so earlier. The grainy images originally produced were very frustrating. When I finished up, HD quality recording in most public places has really put criminals back on their heels.

One of my last cases really highlighted where we had come with technology. The case related to five women from a family group who were charged with stealing a large quantity of meat from a South Auckland supermarket. Amazingly the case relied upon eight CCTV clips, and the evidence of the supermarket's security manager to put what was recorded into context. No product was ever located, as the offending was detected via a random sweep, and none of the defendants admitted any offending. Progressively the clips showed the family entering the supermarket. The Judge was asked to pay particular attention to one of the teenage daughters, who was wearing those black figure-hugging tights that women love to wear. At this point she looked about a size eight, and was kind of attractive in her own way. The next video showed the group in the meat aisle and, the security manager was able to confirm that they were selecting packs of high-quality steak. In all, ten packs were counted into the shopping trolley. The group then went to the top end of the toilet paper aisle and went into a huddle around the shopping trolley. This went on for around two minutes before the group broke apart. The group were then captured on CCTV in various other aisles, before presenting themselves at the checkout. Three of them walked straight through, whilst two produced a bottle of coke and a packet of chips from the trolley being the sum total of what was in it. A $20 note was produced as payment and change was given. The next clip captured the group leaving the store. The clincher was that the relatively attractive defendant in the black tights, now had a rear end the size of a bus, and was closer to a size eighteen I reckon. Not overly out of place for a South Auckland supermarket, but definitely hiding the ten packs of meat. She managed to waddle herself out to the car with the registration plate being captured in glorious high definition. The Judge had no hesitation in determining that the only reasonable inference to draw from what he had seen, was that the group had committed theft and all defendants were convicted. The lawyers were up in arms, and threatening an appeal but it never came to fruition. This case really illustrated, that looks really can be deceiving.

On a personal note looks can also be deceiving. I was beginning to hatch a plan that would see me in a part time role during semi-retirement. It was a role that I was well qualified for and well suited to. It would be an opportunity for me to provide a little more service to the fine folks of NZ. Heck, a certain Government Department would most likely be crawling over broken glass to secure my services. However, that discussion may need to wait for a few more pages. Buckle up, because things could get ugly.

18. I'LL TAKE AN AWAY MISSION PLEASE.

I managed to score a couple of great away missions during my time with Police Prosecutions. One was to a place very few Kiwis have made it to, the Chatham Islands. The other was to Christchurch in the aftermath of the 2011 earthquake.

Chatham Islands 2009

The Chatham Islands are, of course, part of New Zealand; but you had better not come on all righteous to the locals. They refer to us as New Zealand, and themselves as the Chatham Islands. The word 'mainland' does not feature in their vocabulary, and should never be uttered by a visitor. However, like it or lump it, the Chatham Islands are subject to New Zealand law. When I went there in November 2009, there was a solitary Police Officer and a Fisheries Officer. In times of crisis they would team up to help each other out. For a number of years, the Chatham Islands District Court only sat once a year. The crime rate is low, in line with the small population (approximately 600 persons) and most issues seem to be sorted out without the need of a court appearance. However, a challenge was made in terms of the New Zealand Bill of Rights Act 1990, which requires justice to be dispensed without undue delay. As a result, there are now four court sittings per year. The court hearings themselves are staffed entirely from New Zealand, and the courtroom needs to be converted back from being an art gallery, on sitting days. From a Prosecutions perspective, the hearings were generally conducted by a Prosecutor from Wellington comprising a three-day round trip. On occasions, Officers from other Districts were given the opportunity to attend. Some years before, I had made the right contacts for my great colleague Colin, to head down for a five-day trip and by all accounts, he had a tremendous time. In 2009 I managed to score one for myself.

The journey commenced with the short flight to Wellington. Standing at one of the gates at Wellington Airport was an aging Air Chatham's Convair 580 aircraft. Other people were in the small gate lounge, but there weren't any great introductions to be had, so I was left to myself to speculate who was the Judge, Duty Solicitor, Registrar, Probation Officer and Fisheries Prosecutor. Before long we were asked to board. Strangely enough, you were provided with a boarding pass, but not assigned a seat number, so you just sat where you liked. I ended up alongside the Judge. He was very professional, so apart from a brief introduction we didn't talk a lot.

The twin turbo props started up and spun around for a while; and then they didn't. We were all told to get off and go back to the Gate Lounge. A mechanic was called for and we all watched on as the propellers started up, and we noted quite a bit of head scratching, before a big thumbs up was given. Now this wasn't the greatest of starts. We were about to head 800 kilometres into the South Pacific Ocean on the strength of a thumbs up. However, being the good Government employees that we were, we all got back onto the aircraft as we were told, and simply hoped for the best. Thankfully the 1 hour 45-minute flight went without a hitch and we touched down at Waitangi. No, not a wrong turn, Waitangi is also the name of the main township of the Chatham Islands.

After getting off the aircraft, I met up with the local Constable and we waited for my bag. The baggage handler at that time, was a bloke who only had one arm, a Great White found a liking for his other one. It was also legendary that he played on the wing for the local league team, but apparently his fend wasn't up to much. As we were about to leave the airport, I was approached by a stern looking woman, who I was to learn was the Duty Solicitor. True to form, there was no introduction, no, 'How's your father?', no, 'Do you want to get a drink sometime?'. No, all she wanted was the disclosure for the following day's court hearing. My seven files were still at the Police Station, and I had no idea what they involved, so she was asked to call in to the station on her way into town to pick up the paperwork. I could see that some people were indeed taking this jaunt seriously.

We left the bitumen surface of the road into town after 100 metres and the road became limestone dust. I swear that the local cop was driving along at about 60 kph with zero visibility, but he obviously knew the road like the back of his hand. The Police Station and Courthouse / Art Gallery are all part of the same extended building. Next door is the Constable's house. Alongside that, in a separate building is a small cell area, a storage shed and visitor accommodation. There was one slight hiccup when I was heading to my lodging, when the Constable's children mistook me for an escaped prisoner. After dinner I had an opportunity to come up to speed with the files for the morning list. As I recall, there were a couple of domestic assaults, a couple of drink drives and sundry disorder charges. Nothing particularly awkward and no defended hearings. It seemed that cases always sorted themselves out, one way or another.

The courtroom was packed the next morning, as many of the locals took the opportunity to catch up with gossip that they may have missed. Singlets were freshly laundered and gumboots dusted off and arranged at the doorway; this was serious stuff. We kicked things off and a few minutes into proceedings, the power went out. The Judge looked to the Constable, who was the general dogsbody for the morning, and asked how long it might be before power would be restored. The Constable proudly proclaimed that it had been three days on the last occasion. I began to regret volunteering for this assignment. Fortunately, things did spark up again within fifteen minutes and we were underway once more.

One defendant failed to appear and the Judge issued a warrant to arrest him, and directed that the Constable go and find him. They were both back within ten minutes, it seemed that the defendant had simply slept in after a hard night on the juice. Justice was quite efficient around here, as it turned out. My cases were dealt with and then the Fisheries Prosecutor had a go. I think they had about four cases, and they managed to get two vessels confiscated. The word is that the locals go as hard out as they can, knowing that one Fisheries Officer can't cover everyone, and when they are caught, they accept the confiscation as a tax for doing business.

The morning's work was done so everyone adjourned to the takeaway bar next door to celebrate things in style. After chewing the fat for a while, the Constable called me aside, and said that he had been able to borrow the Fisheries boat so we were heading out fishing for the afternoon. Despite the commercial fishermen having their largely unfettered access, we only went offshore for about ten minutes, and were able to pull up sizeable blue cod at will. These were expertly filleted by the Constable and frozen along with paua and kina to be packaged up for my flight home.

The next morning Air Chatham's returned everyone to Wellington without the hint of a misfire and the baggage was nicely secured as well. Some of the cod for the Morgans, the rest to members of the Office, brought to an end a worthwhile and rewarding experience. The Chatham Islands are certainly a location that New Zealanders should get to if they can, just don't mention the mainland.

Christchurch Earthquake aftermath 2011

The Christchurch earthquakes were certainly devastating events. Particularly with the second coming on 22 February 2011, just as the city was getting to its feet after the September 2010 quake. It became clear, very early on for Police management, that local resources alone would not be able to cope under the strain. Other Police Districts were asked to dig deep and find an ongoing supply of Officers who could help out on the ground, in what was known as "Operation Reassurance". It was determined that the people of Christchurch needed to be aware of a highly visible police presence to reassure the community that normality was being restored. Duties included the prevention of looting, and other crimes whilst reassurance offered an ear to listen to, or a shoulder to cry on. Police Prosecutions Service did its part in this Operation. The Manukau office provided a Sworn Officer for a period of a week over a three to four-week rotation. I was the second to make the journey from our office. Upon arrival in Christchurch, we were assigned to a group that would dictate our duties for the following week. Interestingly, and I suppose obviously, a number of older NCO's were teamed together and assigned to various parts of the city, with the mission to be visual and talk to anyone out there. So that we had no misgivings as to the seriousness of the task at hand, on the first afternoon we were driven slowly through the centre of the city (the Red Zone). This was an incredibly moving experience, and one that will remain with me forever.

In groups, we were able to cover the entire city with experienced Police Officers, which enabled the local staff to just concentrate on the high priority business, or indeed have the odd day off to recuperate. Over the next few days our group spoke to literally thousands of people, and it was obvious that our presence was appreciated. I recall speaking to a surfer at Sumner Beach. He told me that he was in the water when the second quake struck. He tried to describe to me what had happened, and he was painfully aware that it wasn't likely scientific, but he said that the water around him moved in blocks. Not moving, as in a wave, he said that the water moved with edges. True or not, I don't know, but that's how it felt to him. Other people I met had suffered great personal loss, but their concern was for others not themselves. Their resilience to the many problems at hand was inspirational. As the week moved on, we were able to move into other duties. The demise of the inner city had meant that the entire social scene had shifted out towards Riccarton, and the increased patronage was becoming difficult for the licenced premises there to manage. We were also able to assist the local staff by attending quite a few 'high priority' calls for service, which assisted in the overall goal of providing a high profile and timely police response.

Most of us were expecting to be inundated with aftershocks. Indeed, the hotel we were assigned to, alongside Hagley Park had cracks in several large windows as a small reminder of the damage caused to the city. Interestingly, I only felt two aftershocks during the week, however several hundred were actually recorded. I had just gotten into bed after a Late Shift and was beginning to doze when I awoke to, what I thought was a freight train coming through the wall at the head of the bed. The other was when we were called to an upstairs restaurant in New Brighton, which was originally recorded as an incident of disorder, but was actually a patron having a heart attack. Just as we exited the lift with the patient, the room began to shake. I'm not too sure if we could have become stuck if we had still been inside the elevator a few moments later.

My service in Christchurch also provided me with an opportunity to catch up with several family members who resided there. Some had witnessed horrific acts, and had property which had sustained considerable damage. It was clear that nerves were frayed. The time spent in Christchurch was quite sobering, but it was also comforting to see that assistance was at hand and people were getting on with the early stages of the rebuild. I am grateful for the opportunity to have been part of this operation and provide whatever service I could. I was even presented with a ceremonial red and black ribbon to wear on my shirt to recognise my service!

19. COMMUNICATION IS ALWAYS THE KEY.

An early lesson learnt from my time with Police, was that communication was the most important factor to be aware of when dealing with others. It is pointless asking someone to do something, if they haven't got a clue what you are on about. This is not just a language issue, as South Auckland is truly multi-cultural, it is more about how things are said. Politeness and empathy go a long way towards achieving a positive outcome.

One example that I believe epitomises the point I am trying to make, was mentioned to me on at least three separate occasions, involving different defendants, Counsel and Judges. The repeated scenario was that a defendant was placed into the dock for either a bail hearing or sentencing. The submissions from both parties, and then the summary and decision of the Judge took over an hour. On each occasion the defendant was returned to custody following the hearing. It was later reported to me by the attending Court Escort Officer, that after exiting the courtroom each defendant had no idea what had happened, and was uttering phrases such as "Did I get bail, boss?" "Did I get sent away? Do you know how long?" "Why didn't anyone ask me what I thought?" It occurs to me, and I'm hoping others also, that in this scenario the most important person in the courtroom was the defendant. It astounds me that so much focus was placed upon the niceties of the court process, that the person being discussed didn't know what was going on. It could be, that each of these defendants was thick, or had switched off from proceedings, but the fact that their first act after leaving the courtroom was to ask the Escort Officer what happened, indicates that they appeared to be interested.

I was very impressed with the way a Judge handled a case I was involved in. A defendant appeared and in a polite and respectful manner, advised the Judge that he did not recognise the authority of the court, and that he was present under duress. Now, Maori sovereignty cases are argued regularly, but there is basically no prospect of success. The Supreme Court has ruled that all New Zealanders are equal, and will be treated under the same rule of law. That doesn't stop people from trying however. In this case, the Judge pointed out that the charge wasn't particularly serious. The defendant could sense that a degree of fairness was emanating from the Judge, and accepted that he had indeed committed the offence. The Judge asked if the defendant had any explanation (not mitigation, as that might have been misunderstood). There was an explanation, but the defendant reverted back to his original position, claiming to not recognise the authority of the court. It was fascinating to see these two proud and articulate men, having a rational discussion without getting angry with each other. The Judge then stepped up his game and slowly and concisely spelt out his understanding of the historical progression of New Zealand law. The Judge pointed out the level of respect that he held for the defendant's argument, but simply stated that it wasn't going to succeed. He then changed approach and spoke of the idiom, "Is this the hill you want to die on?" The penny dropped with the defendant, and he accepted the court's jurisdiction and was sentenced. Sometimes keeping your powder dry for another day can be the best solution to your problems.

I was more actively involved in a Maori sovereignty case, when I saw a huge injustice developing. A teenage Maori male was facing the court on a moderately serious charge. The evidence appeared solid to me. The defendant was accompanied to court by his parents and quite a following of supporters. When the defendant appeared, the parents of the defendant addressed the court, and raised the lack of recognition of the court's jurisdiction, but this time it was in a more aggressive and less respectful manner. The Judge quickly sensed that it could be a problem putting this case to bed without drama. I said that, as it was almost morning adjournment, I could speak to the defendant and his supporters, as they were declining the assistance of the Duty Solicitor, if the Judge had no objection. At the break I spoke quite firmly and directly to the gathered group. I pointed out that it was the defendant who was on trial and subject to any penalty given by the court. I said that I respected the views of the parents, but wasn't convinced that it was appropriate for them to promote their views via their son. After I had finished, they had a private meeting and advised me that they agreed, and thanked me for providing clarity to them. The case then proceeded in the usual manner.

One case that came across my desk made me laugh because I knew the identity of the guy that was involved. There was a notable character around Otara with an unusual name. A couple of young Officers who obviously hadn't had the pleasure of his acquaintance, stopped his car one day. They call this action a turnover, however I don't actually ever recall anything actually being turned over, and certainly not a vehicle. On that point, the Police code for a vehicle turnover is 3T. A request for a vehicle registration check is a QVR. Some smart cookie low life criminal got himself a personalised plate, "3T QVR" to help out the Police I'm guessing. He's just asking for all sort of whoop ass to be unleashed, I bet. I digress however; my guy was asked by the Police for his name, which is their right as he was driving a vehicle on a roadway. He answered in a back blocks accent, words that closely resembled "Stuff you". Now that is a fairly nifty way to get a rise out of a couple of young Police Officers, so they asked him again, this time with feeling. My guy was starting to get a little antsy by now, because he was trying to help so he offers "Can't you guys hear, stuff you". That was too much for our intrepid duo to take and they dived in and locked him up. How the case ever got to me, I don't know, because they all made it to the station, and the charge sheet was completed with the defendant's personal details. You guessed it; my guy's name was "Star Whiu!"

I was a casual observer in court when a miscommunication caused what I thought was a hilarious situation. I was in one of the Civil Courts, which is an unusual situation, but is due to applications for determining ownership of stolen property seized under warrant, being required to be filed in that jurisdiction. Normally I would turn up and make everyone uncomfortable with my uniformed presence, and the Judge would ask for my case to be called first, so I could get out of there and do some real work. On this occasion I saw the name of the rostered Judge and thought that it would pan out as stated. Instead, when the Judge entered the courtroom it was another one completely; chalk and cheese some might say. There wasn't enough room at any of the benches, the QC's and old timers having muscled their way in. I was in the top row of the Jury bench, and it was to give a great view of what was to follow. There was no sign of my case being dealt with, so I hung in there for the long haul. Directly; a case was called, and one of the lawyers was from Auckland and clearly a stranger to these parts, and the identities involved. He greeted the Judge and then went into quite a long diatribe in relation to the case brought against his client. Without access to the paperwork, all I could glean was that the issue had something to do with digital communications, and the internet. It was clear that the lawyer was becoming confused concerning the Judge's apparent lack of knowledge about the issue at hand. Finally, the lawyer exclaimed "But you have written about this in your book?" The Judge looked even more confused, so did I, because I was fairly sure that he hadn't been published, and certainly not relating to this type of case. The penny dropped for me, as I recalled the name of the Judge actually rostered for the hearing, probably on purpose to confront this issue, but of course for some reason or another, a change had occurred. Now being aware of the situation, I was relishing the prospect of seeing how this one developed. The Judge was still confused, and the lawyer finally broke the deadlock by pulling out a copy of the book from his briefcase. About that time everyone else in the courtroom came up to speed. I thought that it was hilarious, and was winding up for quite a belly shaker. Just as well that I didn't, because everyone else was straight-faced with only the very slightest trace of a snigger. That must be the way they roll in Civil Court. It's sad in a way that convention did not allow the others to act upon the lighter side of this situation. I'm sure that lawyer was rueing the day he ever dared fronting up at the Manukau District Court, or at least next time, he would be sure to be certain, as to the identity of the Judge he would appear before.

Some occurrences just make you feel insignificant and cheap. It really went with the role of being a Police Prosecutor. One afternoon I was in my office when I was the District Prosecution Manager at Manukau. I received a phone call from a Judge and he referred to me as "Mike". That indicated to me that he meant business. It was also fairly unusual to be called directly by a Judge. I would go so far as to say that it probably breached protocol, as it was normally a Court Registrar who did all of the scheduling. He told me that a split was on and that he wasn't going to take no for an answer. A demand was made for me to get over there and to make it snappy! He also mentioned something about being sweaty when I got there, but I didn't really know what to make of that! I mulled over a few things, including the mantra mentioned previously of whether this was the hill I wanted to die on. I really should have resisted, many would have, but I decided that I still had a few more battles left before I hung up my boots. I decided that I would call his bluff and I strolled on over.

I certainly couldn't be bothered to raise a sweat though! I entered the courtroom, and saw that the Judge was already on the bench and the defendant was alongside his lawyer. As I made my way to the Prosecution bench, I was handed the Prosecution file. I looked down at the witness list and announced to the Judge that I was calling the complainant to give evidence. I had no idea what the charge was at that point, and I located the charging document and scanned the summary of facts, as the complainant entered the witness box. I had noted that the charge was indecent assault, so I made an application for the courtroom to be closed whilst the complainant gave evidence. As I went through the preliminaries with the complainant, I was able to skim ahead in her statement and saw what I was expected to illicit from her.

This was justice, but not how it was supposed to be conducted. I doubt if any Prosecutor, Crown or Police, had been treated like this up to that point or since, but that's how it happened. The case was solid and had been properly prepared earlier by one of my colleagues, and I was grateful for that. The case progressed as expected, with a couple of witnesses for each side and the defendant was properly convicted. When the Judge adjourned, I wasn't even thanked for my efforts, which I believe were over and above what is generally expected. That really pissed me off, but indicated just how Prosecutors were regarded in some quarters.

One day I was prosecuting a Judge Alone Trial before a Judge who didn't really like me. I suspect that he thought that I was just a little bit too clever for a Police Prosecutor. I don't think that he was alone in that view, it was a recurring theme sadly. During this hearing I was having difficulty with the senior defence lawyer opposing me. On too many occasions he was putting words into his witnesses' mouths, and my objections were largely falling upon deaf ears. For the third, or was it, the fourth time the lawyer transgressed. Not even bothering to raise myself from my seat I let out a "Oh, come on!", not overly dissimilar to the same phrase used on many an occasion by Lleyton Hewitt during his tennis career. You could have heard a pin drop in the courtroom. The young Prosecutor alongside me, to learn the ropes was ready to hand herself into the Custody Unit, already fearing the worse. Was I told off? Of course. Was I repentant? No. Would I do it again? Probably. Did the lawyer come into line? Well, yes, he did (possibly believing that my next approach might be physical). Sometimes you can only get what you want by being a little unorthodox.

20. A TALE OF TWO HIGH PROFILE CASES.

Sometimes, as a big hitter, you had to take on the high-profile cases when they presented themselves. You may hit a home run, or indeed be struck out. Here's what happened with a couple of them.

Are you sure that you're a pilot?

Ben Boyce was forging quite a career in the New Zealand television entertainment industry. After having moved on from co-hosting Pulp Sport, his new show WANNA-BEn, in which he played the titular role, was into its second season, and was performing well. The show was snappy, clever, and most importantly funny. However, on 17 September 2011, Ben and his production team pushed the envelope out too far.

It was standard for the team to try to smuggle inanimate objects, such as alcohol into Eden Park, or Mt Smart Stadium, and everyone thought that their antics were a huge joke. However, things went wrong, when radio jock Bryce Casey was dressed as an airline pilot, and made an attempt to pass through a check point at the regional terminal of the Auckland International Airport. The date is significant, because it was during the Rugby World Cup and the eyes of the world were on New Zealand. It was their stated intent that, if Casey had made it onto the tarmac then he would wave to the camera, and return to the terminal. Judge Andree Wiltens, who ultimately dealt with the case, hit the nail on the head when he said that, 'the stunt did not have sinister motives – but could have had significant consequences.' Don't get me wrong, I can see how the production team thought that the segment could be quite funny, but I think it is all about perspective. Since the attack on the USA on 11 September 2001 the world, like it or not, was a different and more serious place. Travellers at Auckland Airport were regularly being arrested for making light of security checks, by claiming to have explosives or weapons in their baggage. It got so bad at one stage, that I recall a lawyer making a submission to a Judge, on behalf of his client, to the effect that authorities should post signage stating that comments about bombs and weapons shouldn't be made. The Judge rightly told that lawyer that the travelling public should be well behaved, without being told how to.

If an investigative journalist such as John Campbell had become aware of solid information to suggest that a serious flaw existed in our airport security, and he put in place a sting to highlight the issue, I for one could actually accept that, in the ongoing interests of our country. The distinction here was that the attempted breach of security was solely for the purposes of entertainment. It's apparent to me that the production crew didn't give full cognisance to two likely outcomes. The first being New Zealand's global security reputation. Being a laughing stock on an international scale is far worse than a few idiots laughing at a television programme. It might have meant that aircraft departing from New Zealand may have had landing privileges withdrawn by certain countries for a period of time. Imagine how devasting that might have been. The other concern is at a more personal level. At the regional terminal the level of security is not as high as in the Domestic and International terminals. Two Air New Zealand staff were on duty at a desk to check passenger boarding passes, and also to confirm identification of air and ground staff. On this occasion, no fake identification had been produced, as Casey simply told the staff that he had left his pass on the aircraft. Things might have been much worse for the crew if a fake pass was used. This suggests that there seems to have been some insight into this being a borderline escapade. As it transpired, the airline staff were as professional as expected and turned Casey around before notifying security about the attempted breach. If one or both had failed in their duty and allowed Casey access to the tarmac, (which in turn then provides access to both Domestic and International aircraft) dismissals would have occurred. Some might say that would be an appropriate outcome, but I struggle with the fact that the crew put the livelihood of two people at serious risk, solely for the purpose of entertainment.

The group's misdeeds saw six of them charged under the Civil Aviation Act 1990. It was apparent that things could get messy, so I volunteered to guide the case to whatever outcome resulted. I have to applaud Boyce and his colleagues for the professional and responsible approach that they took with regard to the court process. Each engaged experienced Counsel, so that there was no mucking around and showboating. Apparently, Boyce's social media ran red hot initially with anti-police sentiment, which was not surprising as some of his fan base might be described as folks who would get a kick from a monkey being forced to smoke cannabis (that actually happened by the way). Taking complete control of the situation, Boyce pronounced that he would not endorse any comment about the charges whilst they were before the court, and basically kicked the potential problem to touch before it had taken hold.

At every court appearance the group were immaculately dressed and behaved impeccably. Over several court appearances I never observed any joking or laughing, which I imagine must have been quite difficult for these normally jovial characters. Initially, not guilty pleas were entered, which was typical fare as it tends to provide impetus for the disclosure process. In reality, everyone acknowledged that the actions of the defendants were indeed criminal, but not with sinister overtones. When Prime Minister John Key weighed in, he described the stunt as "irresponsible from a bunch of clowns that should know better". There was then some discussion about the potential for Police Diversion, but I soon shut that down, as this incident had caused considerable concern to the 'complainants' Air New Zealand and the Civil Aviation Authority. It was determined that this was a matter that should best be considered by an experienced District Court Judge. There was a potential sentence of up to twelve months' imprisonment and a maximum fine of $10 000 at stake, but that was never likely to happen. All of the defendants entered guilty pleas and made application for a discharge without conviction. Such applications can be granted when the court is satisfied that the direct and indirect consequences of a conviction would be out of all proportion to the gravity of the offence. These applications can be controversial from time to time, with pundits referring to them as get out of jail free cards. There is usually controversy when the offending relates to family violence, contrary to the wishes of the victim, or when the future consequences to a celebrity are not overly significant, but the application is granted anyway. In this case it was obvious that convictions for an airport security related offence would seriously curtail, if not halt, the future prospects of these defendants.

Judge Andree Wiltens did his part though, by making each defendant feel thoroughly ashamed of themselves, commenting that, "All eyes were on New Zealand from overseas to see if there was a security issue. If the escapade had been successful, I'm sure that it would not have been seen as a joke". He apportioned the appropriate levels of culpability to each defendant. He then directed each to complete an assessed term of voluntary community work, and to pay a sum towards the cost of Prosecution. Each defendant completed what was required and discharges without conviction were granted to each.

Following the final court hearing, Boyce approached me and offered his hand in thanks. We spoke briefly about the skill of his new colleague Guy Williams, and that was that.

Boyce later issued a statement and said that he was "very sorry for all the trouble the stunt caused. This was an attempt at humour which we accept was misplaced." A few times over the years since, I have heard the issue raised on radio, usually by Boyce's current bestie Jono Pryor. Strangely, the story is now prefaced with Boyce having dressed up as a pilot, which is not correct. I have been pleased to hear Boyce shut the issue down on each occasion and make no effort to humourize the occurrence. Now that's how a celebrity should behave.

How do you plead Your Honour?

Another high-profile case that I prosecuted did not go quite as well. The Area Manager came cap in hand one day. He advised that a retired District Court Judge had been charged with intentional damage at North Shore, and he was having difficulty finding a Prosecutor. The local staff didn't want to play ball, and it seemed that no Crown Counsel wanted to take the case on, for fear of placing a roadblock on further career progression. Mine had pretty much come to a halt anyway, so I said that I would give it a go. If things panned out well, I could create history I suppose; but it wasn't to be.

On paper, the case looked pretty tight. The Judge lived in an apartment complex in Browns Bay. Constant drama, particularly on the weekends, was caused for the residents when cars parked over the accessway to their carpark. Apparently, this resulted in a fair amount of tension in the area. On this Saturday morning, a sports car had been parked across the driveway which again prevented access to the Judge's home. It was alleged that the Judge lost the plot, and approached the vehicle and keyed its paintwork on a large number of occasions. He denied causing any damage to the vehicle. He pleaded not guilty and a two-day defended hearing was scheduled in the North Shore District Court. Judge Phillips from Invercargill was assigned the case, being as remote from the defendant as possible. The Prosecution certainly had no concerns about the trial process not being fair. This case was going to be decided on the facts.

I commenced the defended hearing by calling the complainant. He of course, did not witness the offending, so was only able to give evidence that his vehicle was undamaged when he left it, and it was scratched in multiple places when he returned to it. He accepted that he had parked illegally but not intentionally so. There was an optical illusion that gave the impression that the access way to the carpark was actually a legal parking space. However, the prosecution accepted that the complainant's parking was not legal. The next witness was pivotal to the prosecution case. He had previously been a panel beater overseas, so he knew vehicles and paintwork. This man was with his wife seated outside of a café a few metres from the complainant's vehicle. He gave clear evidence of noticing the defendant approach the car and saw a hand moving back and forth in an apparent scratching motion. Most importantly, he maintained that was what he saw, despite intense cross examination. At this point I believed that we were in with a real chance. I then called this man's wife, and I wish that I didn't. For a reason, that is still not known to me, she described the seating arrangement such that it was not possible for her husband to have seen what he said that he did. I can only speculate that she got stage fright, and confused her recall, but her evidence placed the Prosecution in a position where the only way the charge could be proven, was if the defendant admitted it. Judge Phillips ruled that there was a case to answer on the basis of our male eye-witness's evidence, but that shouldn't be confused with proof beyond a reasonable doubt.

During the Prosecution case I was able to at least have a little bit of fun. I had previously been told, possibly by Tony T, not to stand for any sledging being dished out by Defence Counsel. You do need to be confident for this to work properly, but what happens is, when you are on your feet examining a witness and you hear quiet utterances coming from Defence Counsel behind you, you immediately sit down. Often the Judge is thinking about what he's going to have for lunch or some other important issue, and he's shaken back into the moment. The usual response is something like "Is everything alright Sarge?". You rise and state "I believe that Counsel wishes to address Your Honour." This normally catches the lawyer off guard so as to flummox about a bit. In this case I was able to execute this ploy twice in a 30-minute period. I know that I annoyed this experienced lawyer immensely, but it was the only trick that I was able to take.

I was surprised when the defendant gave evidence. Clearly, he didn't need to, as our case was never going to reach a standard higher than a case to answer, because of the conflict between the eye-witness testimony. There was a considerable media presence in the room and when I cross examined the defendant, there was a television camera over my shoulder pointed directly at the defendant. There was sweat streaming down my back, but as no one mentioned it to me, it must have just been me who noticed. I tried as hard as I could with the defendant but he was far too long in the tooth and legally savvy to agree to any of the propositions I put to him. I must concede therefore, that he came out on top in that scrap.

Judge Phillips gave his decision and the defendant was acquitted. It was the correct decision based upon the evidence presented during the hearing. I have a personal view about the case, but that matters little. It's what the Judge thinks that counts.

15 The 'Prosecutors' at the South Auckland Police Reunion 2013; Eardley Dijkstra, Trevor Church, Taffy Williams, Michael Morgan, Barry Felton, Tony Tremewan, Colin Graham, Laurie Ohms & Grant Cornwell.

16 With Wing Mate Kerry Petrie at the South Auckland Police Reunion 2018.

21. BETTER WORK STORIES, TOO RIGHT.

I haven't mentioned a royal encounter for a while, but that was about to change, big time. A couple of occasions in 2014 and 2016 really put the icing on top of a career that was drawing to a close.

So, your dad told you to look us up?

One of my Wing mates John, is interested in things royal, and got wind that the Duke and Duchess of Cambridge, that's Prince William and Princess Catherine to the uninitiated, were planning a visit to our shores. The duo was locked in to visit the Royal New Zealand Police College on 16 April 2014. John made representation to the Office of the Commissioner, relying upon the link to our Wing Patron Prince Charles, who had opened the College more than 30 years earlier. To their credit Head Office agreed that interested members of our Wing would be invited to attend, and provided with a guarantee of a meet and greet. Less creditworthy was that those interested had to pay their own way, but in reality, anything more was not likely with budgets constraints and all.

In all nine members of the Wing were able to attend. Some of us met up at Wellington Airport and drove towards Porirua in pouring rain. On the way, some us were able to catch up for the first time since graduation. The rain eased a little upon arrival as everyone met in a room off the main dining hall, to check on the state of our uniforms. The royal couple arrived and the proceedings commenced with the laying of wreaths at the Wall of Remembrance. The Duke and Duchess had minders holding large umbrellas, whilst we stood there in the driving rain, but it was the least that we could do, as we thought about those who had given the ultimate sacrifice for the benefit of the community. We weren't privy to the next phase of the tour, which took place in the gymnasium, and then the parade ground, as the rain eased.

We all took the opportunity to try to dry our sodden uniforms. Thankfully, by the time we were given the nod to take up positions in the main dining room, we were once again looking relatively presentable. Our position was on the eastern wall, coincidently under the large painting of HM Queen Elizabeth II, that has been displayed there since day one. A College representative had been ordered, under a threat of death if failure occurred, to actively direct the couple our way. First up the Duchess was presented to us. Our most senior members greeted her, and explained our connection to her father-in-law. She was simply stunning I must say; however, my opinion on that is not alone. There was a photographer hovering nearby, and after a few words to each of us preparations were underway for a memento to be taken. Now I have to say, because this is quite significant due to what was going to occur next, I had nothing to do with the order in which we were standing. I was number five in a line of the nine of us. In a way it made perfect sense to split our group in the middle, and that's what happened. Next minute I'm standing with the Duchess at my left shoulder and was being told to smile. Smile, I was frigging delirious! Several shots were taken, but somewhat bizarrely I have never seen the photos taken of the group with the Duchess alone. I guess they must be on a hard drive somewhere.

As we finished that photo opportunity, Prince William was led over. Apparently, he had been waylaid by Officers far less important than us, and was probably thoroughly bored by them. He was greeted by our senior members, but the penny didn't immediately drop for him, as he had somehow formed the impression that we were instructors at the College. I think those idiots who had gotten to him before us, must have set us up. Anyway, when it began to look as though our attendance was going to fall flat, the Duchess stepped in. "These men were young Cadets when your father opened this College back in 1981." There was recognition at last, so we settled down to a bit of old home week. Then, what do you know, we were still standing in the same positions held previously. The photographer called for the same split, and once again I had the Duchess at my left shoulder, the Prince alongside her, and my good colleague Russell on the other side. I was like a cat with a bowl of milk. That photograph did do the rounds, and I'm hoping will provide a talking point for future generations of Morgans. This photo is also dual purpose; because if you crop it just right, then it looks as if it was just me with the Duke and Duchess; sorry guys!

After the conclusion of the visit, the nine of us met up at Police National Headquarters for lunch, there being no budget for us to get anything on the house. John spoke up and tested the water for an even more adventurous plan that he had begun to explore. Some of us were wondering whether he could actually pull it off.

What are you lot doing here?

True to his word John made contact with us later in the year. He advised that things had been progressing well. The grand plan was to see whether our Wing Patron, the Prince of Wales, would agree to present our 35-year long service clasps in London in mid-2016. Quite ambitious, but John thought that he had a reasonable chance of success. The Commissioner's Office gave their blessing for John to contact Clarence House. Clarence House is the Prince of Wales home, but also diaries all of his future engagements. Such matters have to be arranged in plenty of time, so John set to work. Sometime later, John was contacted and advised that the Prince was very interested, and they needed to confirm numbers and a date was suggested. Arrangements were also assisted greatly when one of our fold Barry, was appointed as the New Zealand Police Liaison Officer based in London. Having someone on the ground was to be a huge benefit.

In all, eleven of the remaining members of our Wing committed to the venture. For Wendy and I there was a slight logistical issue to resolve. We were already down to meet family for a Mediterranean Cruise in September 2016, and didn't relish the prospect of travelling twice to

Europe in the same year. The problem was solved when we agreed that I should take a decent chunk of long service leave, and Wendy was granted a term's leave without pay, so that we could leave home in early July and return in late September. John kept everyone updated with progress and the date was finalised as Wednesday 13 July 2016 at Clarence House, London.

Being a somewhat sensitive guy, and having no idea of the personal circumstances of some of my colleagues, I reached out to a now Senior Officer I had supervised many years earlier. He in turn contacted the Air Force and quite some time later, I was contacted by a high-ranking airman. It just so happened that an Air Force aircraft was heading to Paris and return over the relevant time frame, and cheap, if not gratis seats, were being offered. By then most of us had booked flights with commercial airlines. However, one of our members had a medical issue which might preclude him from obtaining medical insurance, and the long hauls were probably going to be too difficult. A request was made for him to travel via the Air Force as the range of the aircraft means that it takes 3-4 days to get there, with a number of shorter flights and rest stops. I originally received an email from a Junior Officer who tersely pointed out that the Air Force wasn't a free form of transport for Police. I quoted directly from the high-ranking airman I had dealt with earlier, and I never heard from that upstart again. The end result was that one more comrade was able to attend and I am very grateful to the Air Force for that.

Commissioner Bush was able to schedule a routine supervisory visit to London, and it was indeed appropriate that he should be there as our leader. The New Zealand High Commission also decided to mark the occasion by hosting a function on the top floor of New Zealand House, following the Clarence House function. Invitations to both events were also extended to any family members who wished to attend. My brother Phil was going to be in the UK over the pertinent time period, so he became Wendy and my plus one.

Wendy and I flew initially to Melbourne to pick up our Qantas flight to Dubai. In the Gate Lounge we ran into Wing mate Steve and his wife, who coincidently would be on the two flights with us to London. Our first official engagement was a meet and greet at the Wellington Hotel, Waterloo. This is how I recorded that event in the travel blog that I have maintained over a number of years which can be found at www.morgansoe.wordpress.com

It was great to catch up with some of the guys. Half of whom I haven't seen for 35 years. Things went slightly astray then. The bar was extremely warm so I put my suit jacket over a chair whilst we were given a briefing about the events for today. Of course, when I reacquainted myself with my jacket later my wallet had been lifted from the left breast pocket. Not as bad as it could have been as all of my money cards are kept elsewhere. Just a bit of cash, driver's licence and Police ID. Will hopefully be able to get a replacement licence for Ireland in September. Evidence emerged of one of the bar staff banging into the chair at some stage but unlikely to sustain evidential sufficiency (even the way I review a prosecution file!)

Tried not to let this small setback cause a dampener on events. We had a lovely after-hours tour of the Tower of London culminating in being involved in the 750-year tradition of The Ceremony of the Keys. As our Yeoman stated" You are now part of the history of this place people".

Got back to Bermondsey fairly late. Just getting ourselves sorted now for today's major events.

The event at Clarence House did not start until 1.00pm but it was imperative not to be late, so most of us arrived a little after midday. To while away some time, a few of us wandered up 'The Mall' towards Buckingham Palace. Almost immediately, local Police were drawn to us as our uniforms certainly didn't look quite right. On a number of occasions various Officers had to be told the full detail regarding our presence there. Members of the public began to join in. I recall having my photograph taken with some Spanish teenagers. I'm not entirely sure why, perhaps they thought Tom Selleck was in town.

You just don't stroll into a Royal Residence. Your invitation needs to be presented along with a passport for identification. There was a full security search, fortunately no Police appointments were carried. All cell phones were removed and stored for safe keeping. No cameras were allowed either, the rostered royal photographer would take care of such requirements. The Wing members were separated from the well-wishers. We were shown where the ceremony would take place, and a dry run of the presentation was carried out, with an equerry substituting for the Prince. We were then ushered into the hallway just along from the presentation room. At exactly 1pm we could hear the Prince come down the staircase; we were unable to see him because a curtain had been drawn. After some brief introductions, the ceremony commenced with us being called up in rank order. Prior to leaving New Zealand each of us had been asked to supply a short biography containing certain points of interest about ourselves. At no time did I see the Prince with any notes, but others I asked about this, confirmed that the Prince spoke to each of us directly, about what was on the bio supplied. After I shook his hand and received my award the Prince started talking to me about my love of running. That enabled me to confirm that I had been in London the previous year for the Marathon. He then asked me about my knees, saying that his gave him some trouble. I was able to confirm that mine were okay, but now three years later, sadly one is pretty stuffed. A terrific photograph was taken with the Prince and I laughing with each other as we spoke about our knees, with Commissioner Bush smiling in the background. Following the presentations, we gathered for a photo opportunity at the base of the staircase. Subconsciously I recalled that I had been very fortunate with the photograph taken with the Duke and Duchess of Cambridge a couple of years earlier, so you will find me almost hidden at the back of this one.

Everyone then adjourned to a large reception room for refreshments. Word had reached us that it was unusual for the Prince to provide food and alcoholic beverages for such an event, and that apparently was an indication of the importance he had placed upon this gathering. Prior to the Prince entering the room, we were told by his Personal Assistant that we should remain in our family groups, and that she would ensure that the Prince was able to spend some time with each group. I had to slap my brother back into shape at this point, because he was keen to have a bit of a chat. True to her word, every few minutes the Assistant tapped the Prince on the shoulder and he moved to the next group. At last it was our turn. It was my role to introduce myself again, and then introduce my wife Wendy, as a school teacher, and my brother Phil as a bus driver and union organiser (read into that, a bit of a shit stirrer!). This gave the Prince something to work with, instead of just talking about the weather. Of course, he asked Wendy about the age of her students, whether they were well behaved, and what subjects she taught. The Prince had an in-depth discussion with Phil about Auckland's transport issues and there was a bit of banter about unionism in general. We probably had about five minutes with the Prince and there are a couple of nice photographs to record the occasion (unfortunately the cost to release copyright on them is too excessive, and they are not included in this book). It soon came time for the Prince to leave and to move on to his next engagement. Before he left it was admirable to see him enter an adjoining anti-room, and speak in turn to each member of a string quartet who had been playing tirelessly during the function.

Everyone, except the Prince, regrouped on the top floor of New Zealand House a short walk away. The High Commissioner, Sir Lockwood Smith, spoke of his appreciation for our service, as did the Commissioner. That evening the Wing members and family finished the occasion with a dinner cruise on the Thames. What a wonderful celebration it had been. This is how I recorded it in my travel blog:

Well it's been a day now since a very special series of events. Wendy and Phil have both published their personal and highly informative accounts of the day. There is little I can add to what has already been said. The ceremony at Clarence House was simply amazing. HRH Prince Charles rewarded everyone with a significant meet and greet. It was obvious that he did consider himself to have been involved in our careers and was genuinely appreciative of the 35 years' service each of us have put in. Words cannot adequately describe the emotions of this occasion.

The High Commissioner Sir Lockward Smith excelled himself by hosting us for the "after match" on the 17th floor of New Zealand House. The words of appreciation given by Sir Lockwood and Commissioner Bush were very humbling.

This was followed up with a dining cruise on the Thames. Incredible food and some of the best sights in the world. An amazing finale to a day to remember.

A special thanks needs to go to John Doherty for his foresight and perseverance in making the day possible. The on the spot logistics handled admirably by Sharron and Barry Taylor. The opportunity to catch up with the serving Wing colleagues who were able to attend so far away from home was very special.

I shouldn't need to mention this, but I do so to dispel any rumours. It was slightly disappointing at the time that some social media reports were recording this as a tax payer funded jolly organised by Commissioner Bush. I can categorically state, that we all paid our own way. The Department did designate our attendance in uniform at Clarence House as 'on duty' and therefore paid one night's accommodation. I also made representation to the Department as I didn't really wish to travel for over two months in Europe with my Police uniform, so it was sent back to New Zealand via diplomatic means, and was waiting for me on my desk when I returned.

17 Members of the Prince of Wales 25th Cadet Wing with the Duke and Duchess of Cambridge.

18 It's amazing what a little cropping of a photo can do!

19 Invitation to Clarence House.

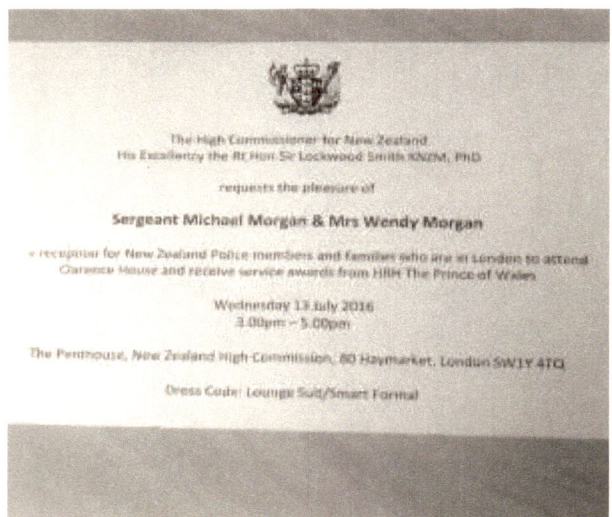

20 Invitation to New Zealand House.

21 With Wendy at the gates to Clarence House.

22 Outside of Clarence House.

23 With Wendy and my brother Phil at New Zealand House.

24 With Wendy at the top of New Zealand House, in front of a beautiful view of London.

22. AND IT ALL CAME DOWN TO THIS…. THE CONCLUSION TO MY HOPELESS OPUS[3].

After returning from long service leave in 2016, I was somewhat unsettled. The travel bug had really bitten hard, and I yearned for something more than just turning up to work each day. Don't get me wrong, the people I worked with were amazing, and hardworking but the job itself just started to get a bit tiresome. My focus returned somewhat when I was placed on a project, to actively target the resolution of cases for defendants remanded in custody. This initiative came from Police Prosecutions Service Head Office, and also required assistance from Corrections and Justice. After a year or so the results were apparently spectacular, with substantial monetary savings and a decent impact upon the size of the remand population. However, by early 2018 I knew that I was nearing the end of my race. Coincidently around this time I also had the realisation that a meniscus injury was also bringing my running career to an end.

I had thoughts for some time about stepping up to become a Community Magistrate. It's a part-time position for around two days per week and involves dealing with

---

[3] Imagine Dragons- Smoke + Mirrors Track 12.

lower-level offences and bail hearings. Strangely, serving Police Officers, practising lawyers, and court staff are unable to be appointed, so you must indicate a willingness to retire or resign to be considered. I say strange, because anyone who asks around the right places, will hear that the current crop of Community Magistrates is not up to much. It's not entirely their fault, as the criminal law and the court process takes quite some time to obtain proficiency in. My enquiries had indicated that they were actively looking for more males, as the current appointees were almost all female. I naively believed that I had something to offer.

In March 2018 applications were called for. It is important to note that this was not for a single position. They were seeking a number of qualified persons to increase the pool of Community Magistrates, as their number had diminished through retirements and resignations. I don't want to be criticised for blowing my own trumpet here, but I will anyway. If they didn't want me based upon my skills, experience, and reputation, then in my humble opinion they weren't actively seeking to appoint anyone. I was able to put together an exemplary application for a position in the Auckland region. A big thank you must go to John, Paul, Alf and Mike for agreeing to be my referees. However, in the end I don't believe that any of you were actually contacted to give your views about me.

It was no surprise when I was shortlisted, and I attended an interview in late May 2018. As far as interviews go it was fairly soft. I got the impression that the panel were either not confident in their role, or simply didn't know what they were doing. The toughest question asked was, "What I would do if my best friend appeared before me on a drink driving charge?" Please, let's get a bit more challenging! I was asked about communication and I gave a couple of examples, including the one written about earlier, where a number of defendants didn't know what had happened to them during a court hearing. Body language indicated to me that the District Court Judge on the panel, didn't like that one, because in a way I was being critical of Judges, but I can't imagine that they are that thin-skinned.

Remember the date, **14 June 2018**, as it will go down in infamy. I received the standard 'You were good, but not good enough' email. I smelt a rat, not of standard pedigree. No, this one was huge, smelly and festering. I made an application for the panel's written report. I take no issue that comments relating to the other applicants were redacted. This is what the panel said about me:

Michael MORGAN

17. Mr Morgan has been a sworn member of the NZ Police since 1982. He is currently a senior prosecutor based in Manukau where he prosecutes a full range of Courts. He has been a Police prosecutor for over 20 years and plans to retire in the very near future.

18. Mr Morgan was an articulate candidate although somewhat overly excited and verbose. His experience in prosecutions equips him well for the role. He gave relevant and informed answers promptly. He was appropriately assertive and displayed a very good approach to decision making. **His current role in the Police makes his appointment to Auckland unrealistic.** *Following a period of time out of the Police he could make an excellent candidate for appointment. The panel rated Mr Morgan's skills and experience against the criteria at 23/30.*

I'm not wildly happy with the last few words of the first sentence in paragraph 18. However, I'm guessing that they would prefer someone a little animated, rather than quiet and unassuming on the bench. The panel gave me the impression of either tiredness, or inexperience during my interview, which left me having to fill in the gaps. I suppose, in hindsight, I should have just twiddled my thumbs.

The most interesting sentence is the one that I have bolded. For anyone who knows anything about writing reports, that sentence should stand out. It is not prefaced by any reasoning, and appears to me to have been inserted as an afterthought. You should also be aware that none of the comments in either paragraph was referred to me in the rejection email.

I commenced dialogue with the Justice Department, in particular the Chief Legal Counsel. We were able to agree that the bolded sentence is the one that led to my rejection. We also agreed that the sentence meant that the panel had concerns relating to my perceived bias and potential lack of impartiality. Shit, that's a bit rich! They appoint Crown Solicitors straight to the benches of the High and District Courts. I don't have a problem with that, because I know and respect many of these appointees but to actively state words to the effect that Police Officers can't be trusted, really ripped my nightie. That was it for me, I simply no longer had any faith in the Justice System.

Now, here is where things become important; take a deep breath and prepare to be shocked. The issue of bias and lack of impartiality **WAS NEVER RAISED WITH ME AT INTERVIEW!** I will state it again, for any disbelievers out there; the issue upon which I was rejected **WAS NEVER RAISED WITH ME AT INTERVIEW!** Now I shouldn't need to say this but I will, in words of one syllable, **THAT IS NOT RIGHT!**

I should really provide a little more information here, to give some more context. A couple of hours after the interview, I was at home after having battled the Auckland motorway traffic. I received a phone call, and I genuinely believed that I was being offered the position. I was caught a little off guard, when the facilitator asked me, whether I wished to be considered for the Hamilton role. There was no explanation at all, clearly this was a stock question. I regained my composure, and stated that the role was designed to be part time in semi-retirement. I indicated that I lived in East Auckland, and that on a bad day the journey to Hamilton could take as long as three hours each way. I was aware that if you were based at a particular court, then mileage and other expense claims could not be made. I finished by saying that I would stick with my application for the Auckland courts. I strongly believe that phone call should never have been made, as it did not relate to any issue discussed at interview.

At that stage I was unaware of this, but there was another Police applicant. The information I have received, is that he was interviewed at some stage prior to me. I know this for a fact, because I was the final applicant interviewed. I'm told that he raised the bias-impartiality issue at interview. I'm not sure why he would do that, but apparently, he did. It is therefore a fact that the panel and the other Police applicant had a discussion concerning that issue. I'm told that he received the same phone call that I did, after the interviews had been completed. He lives further away from Hamilton than me, yet he said 'Yes' to being in consideration for the Hamilton role. That decision is remarkable, and I ask you to digest that, and speculate as to why. Clearly the phone call he received was in context to what was discussed at interview, when my call was not and as such caught me unawares.

So, this is the state of play, the other Police applicant had a discussion with the panel at interview, that I did not have, and gave a decision to a question that had context, to which I was not privy to. Therefore, **THE TWO POLICE APPLICANTS WERE TREATED DIFFERENTLY DURING THE SELECTION PROCESS!** Again, in words of one syllable, **THAT IS WRONG!** The funny thing is, if it can be described that way, that I had a couple of good examples on point to address the bias issue, but didn't as it was never raised. One of them, was when I saved the country thousands of dollars in damages for arranging the release of a young defendant, who had been wrongly remanded into custody, by two consecutive **Community Magistrates**, despite being **bailable as of right**. Did I get any thanks for that? No, of course not. I even formed the impression that the Judge was embarrassed for the inadequacies of his Department.

Consideration has to be given as to why we were treated differently, the options being:

1. It was **intentional.**
2. They **forgot** to raise it with me, with the phone call being an ugly way of trying to put things right.

If the omission was intentional, then the panel showed an unfair bias towards me by actively not providing me with an opportunity to address an issue, that they were about to reject me on, and had discussed with another similar applicant.

If they forgot, then to err is to be human, but there was quite a bit riding on this; so, it can only be described as **incompetency**. Either way I have been treated **unfairly, unreasonably and inappropriately**.

I placed all of this before the Justice Department's Chief Legal Adviser, and sought to commence settlement negotiations. A rejection was received from him and ultimately from his Chief Executive. I had also complained to the Associate Minister of Justice and sometime later, received a response, which I think indicated that I was out of luck.

I complained to the Office of the Chief Ombudsman on 18 July 2018. This process was quite frustrating, as often the only response I would receive as to progress, was when I phoned them. I had quite a number of contacts with them which I won't bore the reader with, but I did have a face-to-face meeting in Wellington on 11 January 2019 with the Manager, Investigation and Resolution Team, which I thought went quite well. However, on 25 February 2019 I received notification that the Office of the Chief Ombudsman believed that it had no jurisdiction to investigate my complaint, that's after seven months people, what sort of review system are you running?

I followed it up with a complaint to the State Services Commission and received a similar response. Their take is that the selection panel is a short-term entity, appointed by the Justice Minister for a particular role, and even though it contained at least two members of the Justice Department, it can't be referred to as a Government agency, and by the way, the panel no longer exists. I even considered making an accusation of gross impropriety, to try to force them back into existence to offer a denial, therefore providing me an opportunity to ask my question. I don't even think that would work.

I want, and clearly deserve the answer to this question, **WHY DID YOU NOT RAISE THE ISSUE THAT YOU REJECTED ME UPON AT INTERVIEW?** It seems that they don't want to answer that question because they know that the answer will cost them dearly. I tried a different approach by contacting the Minister of Justice. I asked whether he would have his new Chief Executive review the decision of the previous Chief Executive. No traction there either; I guess that he has his hands full with maintaining the efficiency of the Justice Department at the level to which they have become accustomed.

I'm hoping that my frustration with all of this has shone through strongly. I've made comment from time to time, that we don't live in North Korea, folks. Our country, according to our swashbuckling Prime Minister, is one of the beacons of hope for the free world. Yet, no one in authority will give me the answer to a simple question. The fact that they won't answer the question gives me licence to say anything I want about them, I guess. Choice, eh!.

Where to from here you might ask? The only legal recourse left is to file a judicial review. Now you've probably gathered that I've lost faith in the Justice System and don't have any prospect of a fair hearing. The loser pays in these types of cases, and I just don't have the confidence to risk it. The only way I could, was if a benefactor stepped forward to cover costs if they were awarded against me. I've now written to the Prime Minister. She grew up in a Police family after all. This wasn't just a slant against me personally, this was a crack at Police Officers in general. Hell, ask the public who they have more faith in, Police or Lawyers? I'm actually surprised that the Police Administration or Association haven't decided to have a bit of a run at them on my behalf.

I received a very prompt response back from the Prime Minister's office. It seems, via her underlings, that I'm not worthy of their intervention, so that door has been shut also.

I saw a news story recently where an Australian woman 'rejected a rejection' from a potential employer. She responded to the rejection by stating that both parties knew that she was ably qualified for the position, so she was turning up anyway to start work the following Monday. I really wish that I had thought of that one!

Anyway, having lost faith in the system, I realised that it was impossible for me to continue as a Police Officer, as I could no longer face working with the Justice Department. In late September 2018, I was sitting on a balcony overlooking Monterosso in Northern Italy, with a cold beer in hand. I was due to return to work in three weeks' time. Not much of a decision really, I looked at Wendy and said that I was going to email Tara, and that I was pulling the pin. "Good for you", she said.

I know that I have to give this up at some stage, but not likely any time soon. The huge festering rat is still present, but it has become even more putrid. Thank you, the reader, for helping me to try to make some sense of all this, as I'm sure that putting my thoughts down in words has helped. What have I learnt from this?

They're just a pack of bastards, **FUCK THEM ALL!!!!**

EPILOGUE

I promise that this really is the end of the book!

Here's the rub. When I put the draft of the book out for editing and review, I received a bit of comment about the previous chapter. There was some concern that it might have been too much of a downer and that it might completely overshadow the rest of my career. No surprise, that it was written with that in mind. I wrote the final chapter in one sitting, and was completely washed out when I completed it. I'm not too embarrassed to say that I shed a tear or two as well.

To finish on a high note then, I'm doing fine and am probably fitter than I have been since my twenties. Wendy and I have planned travel destinations, well into the future. We are not destitute and all things being equal, we have a good chance of making it to old age.

I was proud of my career. I achieved some great things. I had the opportunity to see and do things that others can only dream about. I also had some bad times and there are some memories still around that I wish that I never had.

The people I met within the Police were amazing, so dedicated and hard working. Of course, I met some pricks, and perhaps some of them will get what's coming.... not from me I should add!

To those who still have faith in the law, keep up the good work, and when all is said and done, remember that it is just a job, and heck, you never know, it might just come together to make a collection of great stories!

25 Manukau Police Prosecutions Office 2017.

ABOUT THE AUTHOR:

Mike retired from the New Zealand Police on 12 October 2018 aged 56 years after serving 37 years and 8 months. He declined a farewell befitting that amount of service as he believed it was inappropriate in the circumstances. He hosted a smaller event at his home instead.

He now describes himself as a full-time athlete (4 RPM classes, several long walks, an afternoon of tennis and a couple of standard gym workouts per week are a testament to that) and also a travel blogger. (www.morgansoe.wordpress.com).

Mike's wife Wendy is a semi-retired primary school teacher. His eldest son Jonathan is a senior quiz writer and presenter. His youngest son Anthony is a senior tax accountant with a multinational firm.

26 Farewell from the New Zealand Police

PHOTOGRAPHIC ACKNOWLEDGEMENTS:

1. Reproduced with the permission of the New Zealand Police Museum.
2. Reproduced with the permission of the New Zealand Police Museum.
3. Reproduced with the permission of the New Zealand Police Museum.
4. Reproduced with the permission of the New Zealand Police Museum.
5. Reproduced with the permission of the New Zealand Police Museum.
6. Reproduced with the permission of the New Zealand Police Museum.
7. Photographer unknown.
8. Reproduced with the permission of the New Zealand Police Museum.
9. Photographer unknown.
10. Photographer unknown.
11. Photographer unknown.
12. Photographer unknown.
13. Reproduced with the permission of Wendy Morgan.
14. Reproduced with the permission of Gerald Shacklock Photography.
15. Reproduced with the permission of Cathy Ahuriri.
16. Reproduced with the permission of Cathy Ahuriri.
17. Copyright New Zealand Police Gareth Davies.
18. Copyright New Zealand Police Gareth Davies.
19. Reproduced with the permission of Wendy Morgan.

20. Reproduced with the permission of Wendy Morgan.
21. Reproduced with the permission of Phil Morgan.
22. Photographer unknown.
23. Photographer unknown.
24. Photographer unknown.
25. Reproduced with the permission of Ivan Tarlton.
26. Reproduced with the permission of Wendy Morgan.

www.ingramcontent.com/pod-product-compliance
Lightning Source LLC
Chambersburg PA
CBHW030617220526
45463CB00004B/1327